BRAND WITH PURPOSE

FIND YOUR PASSION, STAY TRUE

TO YOUR STORY, AND

ACCELERATE YOUR CAREER

IVAN ESTRADA

FOREWORD BY PRINCESS SARAH CULBERSON

BRAND WITH PURPOSE

PAGE TWO

Cataloguing in publication information is
available from Library and Archives Canada.
ISBN 978-1-77458-041-7 (hardcover)
ISBN 978-1-77458-042-4 (ebook)

Page Two
pagetwo.com

Edited by Emily Schultz
Copyedited by John Sweet
Proofread by Alison Strobel
Cover and interior design by Peter Cocking
Interior illlustrations by Michelle Clement
Printed and bound in Canada by Friesens
Distributed in Canada by Raincoast Books
Distributed in the US and internationally by Macmillan

21 22 23 24 25   5 4 3 2 1

IvanEstrada.com

CONTENTS

FOREWORD

*As we honor ourselves, we can inspire
others to honor themselves. And then, what kind
of difference can we make in the world?*
PRINCESS SARAH CULBERSON

WHEN I MET Ivan through our mutual friend, I felt like I had known him my whole life. Even though we are from very different backgrounds, we both grew up feeling we didn't fit in. We shared similar struggles connecting with our identities. It took courage for me to work through my challenge of being adopted and for Ivan to face his challenge of being Latino and LGBT. That journey of overcoming fear and reconnecting with our parents is what bonded us in a deep, heartfelt way. We are both proud of our commitment to continuing education and self-development. This self-reflection is what creates a powerful story.

An author myself, cowriting my memoir *A Princess Found* was my effort to create a resource for others as I shared my story of connecting to my ancestry and community in Sierra Leone and the family

I grew up with in the United States. My book has opened so many doors. Beyond what I could imagine, so many different readers have told me how they relate to my story and feel a connection and feel empowered. Even though I started off being silent and afraid to share on social media, as I have developed my social media presence in the last three to four years, I see how it is a way to connect with so many beautiful people. I meet people from all over the world and have even found cousins through sharing my story. As a late bloomer to social media, I now see how much impact I can have and wish I had started sooner. A recent video interview I did got almost 15 million views and that attention helped raise an unexpected amount of money for my foundation, Sierra Leone Rising. Connections on social media show that so many people support my commitment to our projects, which include building wells and providing access to clean drinking water.

Ivan is a pioneer, a self-made entrepreneur harnessing the power of social media to launch and develop his successful real estate career. He is an inspiration. He is a light, a resource who lifts other people up, someone who cares about the world. He has so many accomplishments and is humble, kind, and generous. Ivan shares his story of self-discovery so that others can identify patterns that shape who we are. It is so wonderful that *Brand with Purpose* gives the reader inspiration from interviews, case studies, and questions. I wish I'd had this book early on, so I could have been better with social media and networking. I am still learning how to manage a team. We all need the support of a team to help move things forward. Ivan shares with us how we can get a team to support us so we can all fulfill our dreams, so we can make a difference in the world.

Ivan takes the reader on a journey inwards, to know who you are, so that you can attract support and growth for your career. He shares questions and insights from his personal journey that helped him become more courageous. This book gives readers access to inspirational stories from leaders and coaches, and it is such a special resource. There is something powerful about having all this information in a book. There are hours of material you can sit with and reread whenever you want. You can go at your own pace and discover your power as you do your own self-reflections.

I hope you become more courageous, honor yourself, let your light shine, and dream bigger on what a difference you can make in the world.

PRINCESS SARAH CULBERSON

PREFACE

SEE WHAT our experts say about what "brand with purpose" means to them:

"What we call a brand can only exist if you know what you believe in. How can I use the skills and gifts I have to be of service to the values and causes that mean something to me? How can I use myself in the furtherance of my beliefs? That's the purpose. Each and every one of us came into this world with a purpose. Our first job is to figure out what that purpose is and our second job is to use our skills in furtherance of that."

WILSON CRUZ, actor and producer of *Star Trek: Discovery*, *Visible: Out on Television*, and *My So-Called Life*; LGBTQ activist and national spokesperson with GLAAD

"There are choices that I make to protect [my brand]. There are certain shows I won't do; certain kinds of certain things I won't do as far as my career goes. [A brand], it's a valuable asset. I may not look like a punk rocker, but I have a punk rock heart. I was born contrary."

BELINDA CARLISLE, singer and musician; lead singer of the Go-Go's; author of *Lips Unsealed*

"Whatever you are representing, make sure you are so proud of it... Every individual, we have something incredibly dynamic that the whole world wants. That purpose represents who you really are, and put out that brand. Focus on that, build your brand, reach that zone, and put out more product under that brand. That brand is representing the entirety of who you are."

MARK BATSON, Grammy Award–winning music producer, musician, and songwriter for albums with Eminem, Alicia Keys, Beyoncé, LeAnn Rimes, and Anthony Hamilton

"What are you, what are your dreams? Write out everything you want. Start sharing it with people who support you and your community."

PRINCESS SARAH CULBERSON, dancer, actor, philanthropist, educator, and author of *A Princess Found: An American Family, an African Chiefdom, and the Daughter Who Connected Them All*

"Brand with purpose has a top-down and inside-out approach for me. You [are] creating a brand for something that you want to inspire others to do, or [something] that you were inspired by. My brand has two folds... Paying tribute to my mother. And at the same time, I wanted to inspire others to also appreciate sustainability and eating healthy food."

CATHERINE AN, philanthropist and CEO of An Family restaurants, known for Crustacean, Tiato, and An Catering

"Have a purpose. Be intentional. Be clear about what you want and what you're putting out in the world. It's going to be more effective and you'll have more success. You'll also feel more fulfilled."

BRITTNEY CASTRO, leading finance expert, professional speaker, and entrepreneur with a passion for educating individuals on holistic financial planning strategies

"Doing something with a reason. There's a reason why you're doing something with your life. You're not just doing it because you're doing it. You're doing it because you love it. You're doing it because it can help."

PAUL MENDOZA, lead animator at Pixar for Oscar-winning films such as *Coco*, *Toy Story 4*, and *Ratatouille*

"It's a process of remembering and getting down to the pure essence of what that is and so that you can key in on it and communicate that singular message over and over again without all the noise that's obscuring it."

LIZ MARIE, brand strategy expert and creative director for small businesses and Fortune 100 companies

"Branding is so much about who you are and what it's supposed to mean and the ramifications of that. I think you have to be really sure of who you are as a person before you can figure out what your brand should be. It has to come from internally to be able to really come across and resonate in an actual way that's meaningful."

ANISHA MANCHANDA, lawyer and VP of development and production in TV and film

"Have an honest story. One that's going to resonate with the public. I don't want any smoke and mirrors."

PHIL LOBEL, public relations and media consultant for stars such as David Copperfield, George Michael, and Tony Robbins

"Branding is connecting. Branding with a purpose is connecting with the world, your ideas, how you give back."

JOSÉ CABRERA, therapist and artist influenced by comics and his urban upbringing; author of bilingual children's books

INTRODUCTION

Welcome to *Brand with Purpose*

WHAT IS the concept "brand with purpose"? Having purpose is having an internal drive, sensing that fire inside, that oxygen that makes you feel truly alive. You can have "small purposes" that add up to a bigger drive. It takes some soul-searching and honesty to uncover pieces of you that may have been hidden. Knowing your purpose is knowing what you want to be remembered for.

This book will help you uncover your purpose to help you drive your journey of branding. Brand with purpose is having clarity in broadcasting the message and being seen for your gifts in a way that serves a greater good.

Not having purpose is more obvious: you feel lost, disconnected, you have a vague outlook on life, you don't feel connected to anything greater than yourself. Branding without purpose is broadcasting a message that doesn't feel authentic to you. I have experienced this lack of purpose and I had phases in my life where I had to redefine my purpose, because the old me needed a new journey.

Why did I write this book? This book is a collection of wisdom I wish I'd had when I was younger, and it is a book I want to give to younger generations. Through my twenties I was driven by money, status, and external validation. I worked without a greater purpose. In the last few years I have found a larger meaning for my career. I have learned I have more to contribute than my success in the real estate industry. Right before my nephew was born, my sister told me she wanted me to be my nephew's guardian should anything happen to her and her partner. That was a life-changing moment for me. It dawned on me that my Peter Pan ways had to go and I am now responsible for the well-being of loved ones and the next generation. Becoming an uncle was a very big moment in my life, and I want my nephew to grow up in a world where there are more trailblazers and mentors (like you!) for whatever career and community he chooses to build. This book is for you if:

- you are an entrepreneur looking for a diversity of wisdom
- you are interested in a workbook to help you with personal growth
- you felt different and didn't fit in
- you lacked mentors in your community who were working your dream career
- you lacked mentors who looked like you
- you're creative and looking for a career that might be outside the box

This year, a jewel of a business deal came my way that rewarded me for my branding. I secured the listing of the multimillion-dollar home where Dolly Parton lived for three years and wrote her movie *Christmas on the Square*. The owner, who could have chosen any real estate broker, said he remembered me from years ago when I hosted an open house that he visited. He was impressed by our conversation about music and I stood out to him because I was also a singer. He couldn't remember my name, but he found me through an Internet search. He wanted the right person, someone who was passionate about music, to represent this special home. A seemingly unimportant conversation I had with a visitor at my event, combined with my branding efforts that had put me at the top in an Internet search, created this business opportunity years later.

Like a Swiss Army knife, this book has a variety of tools for you to use. On your journey to a successful career or business, sometimes you want to focus on one tool and other times you want many choices or a combination. With the tools you'll acquire from this book, you can be thoughtful and proactive and respond to situations with agility. You can read this book quickly as an overview or dive deep to focus on one chapter that is most relevant to your current projects. Most importantly, have a notebook or journal where you do the exercises. You need to do the exercises to get the full benefit of this book: a transformation that will send you on a personal journey. Please don't read more than one chapter a day when you're ready to do the work. Let the information simmer and see where it leads you.

While I am sharing my personal story of career successes and inspiration with you, I am also sharing with you new interviews and research from my diverse community of friends and colleagues who are amazing leaders in their professions—whether marketing, real estate, or entertainment. These case studies with an "insider's look" will help you learn the key components of their success. There are also exercises so you can do your own assessments and investigate resources for further learning.

As a successful entrepreneur, I hope to help you accelerate your career path just as mentors and other colleagues have helped me to learn. I am continuously learning, so please check the book's website (BrandWith.com) and social media for the latest updates. This published book is a foundation for Brand with Purpose, which serves as an independent course of "Branding 101," and the Internet-based updates create the continuing education to take you to the next level. If you want to go further and begin producing videos, you might start with chapter 5, "Personalizing Video," which is an introduction to producing your own videos. And if you want to go even further on that topic, please take a look at my course Brand with Video.

I'm very interested in the "young" entrepreneur because it's what I became, so this book is for you if you're newly thinking about entrepreneurship in high school or in your twenties. It is also for you if you're mid-career and looking for a new path as an entrepreneur. Depending on where you are in your journey, you might reread certain chapters at different times to get a different insight to help you. I hope this book is a good reference to inspire you no matter where you are. Whoever you are, this book can lead you on a journey of self-discovery like the one I experienced.

What is a "brand"?

Definition: a brand is a name, term, design, symbol, or other feature that identifies one seller's good or service as distinct from those of other sellers.

Or, if you're not currently selling a product, it is your reputation, your identity in the community, what people say about you when you're not in the room.

Building a brand is as important for a large corporation like Marriott as it is for a real estate agent, a performing artist, or a local flower shop. It creates a sense of trust when others know what to expect of you and your company. This book will help you create your unique, authentic brand with exercises that help you reflect and discover the essence of you. Many of us look for external branding experts to guide us by telling us what they think our brand should be, when the answers are to be found in our own experiences, challenges, and obstacles. Once you have explored and defined your "purpose" with the help of this book, you will be in a better position for a branding expert to help you. Or, if hiring branding experts is not in your current budget, this book can empower you to take charge of your own branding efforts.

I emphasize "purpose" in this book as it's the main driver in guiding you to find your authentic voice for your brand. Whatever industry you choose to work in, you will have a target audience made up of the people you are best suited to serve. And really, we can't please or serve everyone, so we might as well be true to ourselves, so we can have more authenticity and joy in our work. Throughout life, we sometimes forget who we are, get swayed by the opinions of others, lose our ability to speak our truth, or lose track of who we are really meant to be. My goal is to help you create a timeless brand that builds loyalty, influence, and—most importantly—a "brand with purpose."

How to use this book

Each chapter can be used separately like a "choose your own adventure," and you are welcome to flip to the topic you are most curious about at the moment. While I have organized this book into themes, I encourage you to pick what you want to learn first. As my personal success has been guided by my gut instinct, I encourage you to "trust your gut."

Timing is everything. If you're just starting out, go ahead and start at the very beginning. Maybe you are a tactile learner and don't know what you want to learn, so try flipping through the pages with your eyes closed and see where your fingers stop to determine which pages to read. If you recently listened to a podcast or are thinking about a specific topic, go to a chapter that focuses on that theme and see how learning about the same topic from different angles can help you discover what direction you want to take for yourself.

For example, let's say you're about to launch a product with an event. Please be sure to read chapter 11, "Life's a Party: Building Community." Events are essential to how people see your brand, your company, your products. A colleague of mine says, if you don't understand what branding is, your brand is how someone feels when they are at your event, the vibe of your party. Marketing is the invitation, getting people to come to your party. You need all aspects of that successful event: the invitation to get people to come, and a successful event so people will come back to another party and continue to support your brand.

Let's say you're already establishing your career and you're curious about building a team. Please go to chapter 7, "Building a Team, Expanding Your Brand," where you'll get wisdom from my personal mentors early in my career, Fran Hughes and Rick Dergan. With their combined experience and my research, you'll get several lifetimes of experience to help accelerate your progress. This chapter is especially helpful for those who work in real estate. It is also relevant to anyone looking to assess their own skills and develop an organization that works harmoniously. If I knew these lessons early on, I might have been able to prevent some of my mistakes in hiring and partnerships. However, the mistakes I made have become gifts, lessons for me to share with you so you have a larger perspective. People who aren't a match for your business can be referrals and great assets to someone else's success. Learning to assess people's personalities and strengths will help you work better with your people, so you can be the best leader, and they can be your best team.

Or perhaps you've been an entrepreneur and are looking to switch to a new industry or role. Go to chapter 14, "Pivoting," to help learn how to carry your strengths to your new destination. Or perhaps you want to figure out what your new career might be. Learn from my community of successful colleagues and see what considerations can help guide your way.

Branding takes time. It is a personal and professional journey. It takes time to do the personal investigation of what values and vibe you want to put out there. It takes time to develop the media and experiences to communicate your message. And it takes time for people to see your reputation and message be amplified by the like-minded community you build. No matter how you go on your journey, let excellence be part of your brand.

Some of the inspiration I share with you are case studies of leaders I admire, quoted from major publications or their own podcasts and websites. Then I looked within my own network of friends and colleagues and realized I had so much wisdom from these personal contacts that would be new to share with you. The interviews and wisdom quotes I have collected from my community are so rich that I could not include everything in this book. These experts have incredible careers and experiences, and more about their careers can be found on their websites, listed at the end of this book, under References. Sometimes their wisdom quotes are sprinkled across several chapters. For more information about my community of inspiring leaders, please check out their interviews with me and subscribe to my podcast, *Brand With Podcast*.

Thank you for being courageous as you seek to find your entrepreneur path and for letting me be a guide in helping you find your strengths and resources. Stick with me through this book and be sure to read the last chapter, "Reflections," where I share how writing this book has changed me. And I would love to hear how this book has changed you!

Note: Where I mention people by their first name only, I have sometimes changed the name to respect the person's privacy.

1

WHAT'S YOUR STORY?

People don't buy what you do,
they buy why you do it.

SIMON SINEK

Finding my stories

WHEN MY nephew Luca was about to be born, my sister, Vianett, asked me to be his legal guardian if anything were to happen to her and her partner. We were at my parents' house, and my sister rarely has serious conversations with me. She had her intense face on as she looked me in the eye and asked, "Can I count on you?" Previously, Vianett had called me Peter Pan, and this was her way of asking me if she could trust me. It made me realize we weren't kids anymore and that I was going to be responsible for another human being. Of course, I wanted nothing to happen to my sister and her partner. It was the first time I saw that my little sister wasn't a kid anymore, that I was making a promise to a mother. It was an awakening. It was a change of roles. As my little sister was stepping into parenthood, I realized I had to grow up too. My sister was a mirror of me, a reminder that I was not going to stay young forever. Vianett had been my teammate in my childhood, and now she was asking me to step up and be on her team, to keep my promise that I would be there for Luca.

When I was holding my nephew in the hospital, I heard my sister's conversation with me loudly replaying in my head. I needed to clean up my life to keep my promise. Every time I see Luca now, as he is growing, I see a piece of my sister in him. He is a happy kid and not shy about his feelings, with great authenticity and no filters. I see an opportunity to teach him everything I know. I want to be a good example. I want to show him what is possible for him. I want the world for him. I have been more aware that I'm leaving the planet for him and the next generation. It reminds me how I had a beautiful upbringing with my parents and family. I want to groom him to take over my business. In deep, true love for him, if he chooses not to take over my business, I want to support him in his path, no matter what he chooses.

Thinking of Luca reminds me of how my sister supported me in my first ventures of entrepreneurship. Even as a six-year-old, I knew my parents did not have much money to spend on toys. And I knew that college was expensive and we might not be able to afford it. My Mexican immigrant parents worked hard, but I knew I wanted to earn money and save it. So I recruited my sister to knock on our neighbors' doors and sell our drawings for two dollars each. I knew we were cute kids; we told people we were saving money for college, and we were so excited that people actually bought our drawings! It's not that the drawings were so excellent, it was that I had a purpose and a story that people bought. I brought home the money we had raised, so proud to give it to my parents so we could put it into a savings account. I wanted better opportunities and I was planning to improve my future. My neighbors gave me their two dollars to support this goal. Instinctively, I have been good at marketing and selling ever since I was a kid.

While writing this book, I went through my childhood stories and realized there is a through line with my entrepreneurial adventures: I have always been a good salesperson. And through all my stories, I displayed these strengths: creativity, leadership, and hard work. Once I put my mind to something, I would recruit my sister or a friend to help me with my project. No one is successful without help or mentorship. Even when I had a solo project, my sister still helped me stay out of trouble!

My career success is a collection of a lot of things. I was the first person in my family to attend college. I was one of only three Latinos at my accounting school. In real estate, I built my brand in the Beverly Hills market. After three years, I studied and got my broker's license because it was another branding opportunity to show I am at the top of my game and education matters to me. It was a symbol of commitment to the real estate profession, to show my clients I am serious. I'm growing my team to be a billion-dollar sales team in annual sales. Commercial and development is the next step for my residential sales team. I've been doubling my personal sales year after year for the last five years, to be a million-dollar producer.

As of May 2021, I am part of a selected cohort with a competitive continuing education program at Stanford University, the Latino Business Action Network, with a lifetime membership after the six-month program. Attaching the Stanford name to my brand shows my commitment to professional development and leadership. My vision is to expand "Brand With" to include coaching and public relations as well as an annual conference where people can come to get inspired. Please visit BrandWith.com to find out about the latest events and resources I am developing for you.

Find your story

We all have a story. It is helpful to look at your childhood strengths and experiences. See what has stayed with you as you traveled on your journey in entrepreneurship and branding. It is this story that gives you your authenticity and creates trust with your audience.

For example, I want my name to show up at the top of an Internet search when someone is looking for a motivational speaker or a leading entrepreneur. I want the Internet to show that I am making a difference. Could I become the Latino version of Oprah Winfrey, Tony Robbins, and Jay Shetty, influencing all kinds of entrepreneurs? I want to help younger people develop their successful journey without unnecessary obstacles. My mentorship efforts are aimed at helping people to be proud of who they are and their uniqueness.

Your purpose can come from one moment or experience, and it can start with a smaller project that repeats and makes a bigger impact as you grow it. Your purpose can change over time, and it can stay local or go bigger. Examine your personal story and start something that shares your purpose with a community. I am a big fan of art, and often sketch in my journal. So when I saw this inspirational story from a big-hearted 10-year-old who is spreading the gift of art kits, I had to share my thoughts with you.

Case study: Chelsea Phaire, founder of Chelsea's Charity

Chelsea Phaire has wanted to start a charity since she was seven years old. Since August 2019, at the age of 10, she has sent over 1,500 art kits to children in foster homes, homeless shelters, women's shelters, and schools affected by gun violence. At her birthday party, she used the occasion to ask for donations to send her first 40 kits to a homeless shelter in New York. Chelsea's inspiration is a story of how art helped her when she was down. When she was eight years old, she lost her swim instructor, who was also a close friend, to gun violence in the middle of their swim lesson. Art became her therapy, and she wants to share it with other kids who have been affected by trauma. With the help of her parents, Chelsea has even traveled to meet some of the kids who received her art kits and shared her art tips with them.

What can you rely on?

"Art is important to me because no matter how bad I'm feeling, or if it's sunny or raining, my art supplies are always there for me... No matter what happens, know that art is a start."

YOUR INSIGHT What is something you consistently enjoy, or turn to? This can be the foundation of your purpose.

Share your dream

"I feel good inside knowing how happy they are when they get their art kits... I have definitely grown as a person because of this. Now my dream is to meet every kid in the entire world and give them art. Who knows, maybe if we do that and then our kids do that, we'll have world peace!"

YOUR INSIGHT How can you take your efforts and connect them to a bigger dream that you can share with others?

Support for mental health

From Chelsea's mom: "Art therapy is being prescribed a lot more to support the mental health of young kids, especially those with social and emotional deficiencies."

YOUR INSIGHT What is meaningful to your mental health? Who specifically do you want to share it with?

Use your story to differentiate

Staying true to your story is a way to stay above the competition and keep your audience engaged. When I met GT Dave at a party and learned about his company, I was so inspired. Kombucha has an odd taste and doesn't appeal to everyone, and yet he's carved out a market due to his story. As a pioneer, GT Dave has been convincing people to try kombucha and become fans since the 1990s. That kombucha helped his mom combat cancer is the story of why he started his company, so that he could share its health benefits and make his kombucha accessible to others. That story reflects such a strong mission, a strong purpose, that no competition can take it away from him or his company.

Case study: GT Dave, CEO and founder of GT's Living Foods

GT Dave was the first to market kombucha in the United States. From his origins with home-brewed kombucha, he rebranded his company as GT's Kombucha and then expanded it to a larger brand called GT's Living Foods, which is worth over $900 million, and he owns 40 percent of the kombucha market. In his first year, he was selling some 20 cases a day to health food stores around Los Angeles, sometimes with his mom as his marketing spokesperson. With his research into the Eastern kombucha history, he has kept to his high level of quality and refused to pasteurize his products, despite a controversy in 2010 that threatened the kombucha market. To this day, his brand uses the same batch of yeast and bacteria his parents received and that started his first commercial batch. GT Dave has not strayed from his small-batch formula and quality despite stiff competition from bigger brands owned by Pepsi and Coke, who make less expensive versions. He has turned down deals to sell his company since those deals would have required him to give up control over his formula. In 2016, GT Dave expanded his line by acquiring a family-owned business called Tula's CocoKefir, fermented coconut water. The genesis of CocoKefir is similar to GT Dave's story: parents created a drink they hoped would help their autistic daughter. Buying a company with a similar story made sense for GT Dave's brand. He has also branched out into other drinks and continues to grow the business.

Have a story with meaning

"If your claim to fame is that you're in amber bottles, or you're three cool hipsters behind this product, and that's it? Your days are numbered, in my opinion. Our saving grace is that at the end of the day this company truly is an extension of me... I refuse to let someone else who just joined the party change the narrative."

YOUR INSIGHT What is distinctly and personally you in your product or business?

Protect your product

"I was a one-man show. I brewed, bottled, delivered, labeled—you name it... This product was something really special and something that very much had aspects of me in it, and I wanted to protect it."

YOUR INSIGHT No matter how your competition might drive the market or dilute the quality, what can you do to protect your brand?

Be bold with risk

"A lot of companies our size shy away from risk. I think that's what kills the entrepreneurial spirit."

> **YOUR INSIGHT** Playing it safe means staying with the crowd. Taking risks means growth and innovation. How can you be bolder when taking risks?

RISK AVERSE
SAFETY
PLAY IT SMALL

RISK LOVER
INNOVATION
PLAY BIGGER

No limits

My friend and wellness doctor Jonathan Leary is a visionary and chiropractor who wanted to reach a wider audience beyond his solo medical practice. He found a great location for his social wellness club, Remedy Place, on Sunset Boulevard, a prime location with easy access for clients in the Hollywood Hills. However, it was a parking garage space that needed to be renovated, an unusual frame for a wellness clinic. Partnering with an architecture firm helped him conceive and build out a social club vibe that he originally could not see. There were no limits to what he could do with the space. He knew he wanted it to be the opposite of a typical doctor's office, which can drive up people's heart rate. He decided he wanted a "darker, sexy, and unconventional" space that helps people on their path to wellness. The story of his branding and his unique interior design draws curiosity about his business.

Wisdom quotes from Jonathan Leary, CEO and founder of Remedy Place

Think of your own way

"I think if people just double down on trying to find out what they really love... you can be successful in anything... Because I never followed any rule book or had a mentor that told me, 'This is how you're supposed to do it,' it forced me to think of my own way based on what my gut feeling was... I needed to create a club atmosphere that can make people feel social but cut away all the temptations and toxins. I needed Remedy Place to look like a place [where] someone would actually socialize."

YOUR INSIGHT Are there rule books in your mind that limit your thinking about how you're supposed to do something? What if you had no limits?

Think big and dream big

"The more that I surrounded myself with big thinkers and big dreamers, it allows you to feel more normal and that your dreams can't be too big."

YOUR INSIGHT Who do you know that thinks and dreams big? How can you spend more time with them? And if you know you want more positive influences, how can you support yourself in thinking and dreaming big?

Find your strengths

My mom says I have always been good at math, so that's probably why I studied accounting in college. Maybe I knew unconsciously as a kid that having money would give me opportunities I didn't see in my community, and that motivated me to practice math. My mom was my first teacher in managing money. She had a clothing business where we sold clothes out of the trunk of her car. I remember going every Saturday morning to Downtown LA's fashion district to buy from the wholesalers. My mom had a little notebook where she kept track of the accounting. We would drive around to her clients, who were primarily from the Latino immigrant community and worked lower-wage jobs and other domestic work. These were women who did not have credit and could not easily buy clothes for themselves and their families. Some worked multiple jobs and did not have access to a department store. My mom's business provided an invaluable service for them. It was more than just clothing; it included credit and personal shopping services as well.

With my mom's personal shopping business as an early example, I bought candy at the discount stores and sold it for a profit at school. When there were collectible cards that were being traded at school, I found packs of those at a discount and broke up the packets to sell single cards at a profit too. To this day, it doesn't matter how much money I make, I love to find a deal. I think everyone loves to find a deal. And if you can find a deal for someone else, it makes a win-win for everyone.

Another strength I have is that I'm a morning person. Even as a kid, I was an early riser. That's my best time to learn and to study. In these quiet hours of the day, I love listening to podcasts and inspirational videos for motivation. One of my favorite coaches is Jay Shetty, and I want to share some of his inspirational quotes to help you identify your story and your strengths.

Wisdom quotes from Jay Shetty, storyteller, podcaster, and former monk

Know your strengths

"The one way to know your strengths is to ask yourself, 'What do you do that you feel the most confident doing?'"

YOUR INSIGHT What do you feel most confident doing? Is that something you want to continue doing? If not, what qualities about this strength can you transfer to another skill you want to excel at?

Find your passion with compassion and embrace polarities

"[A piece of] real monk wisdom [is] that life is actually about embracing polarities. It's actually about doing a dance and knowing which way to go at the right time. I believe as much in strategy as I do in sincerity. And I believe as much in generosity as I do in generating value for myself. And I believe as much in giving as I do in growing. As soon as you start to say no, it's either-or, you have to choose, that's where we lose a part of ourselves. That's why I add that compassion to passion. I know a lot of people who do what they are passionate about but actually lack meaning and purpose in their life because they haven't turned it into service."

YOUR INSIGHT What is a passion you have that can include a community service component? Does that spark a fire in you? *Flip that coin*: Is there a service you like to provide that you can transform into something that generates income for you?

Stories from your family or culture

A treat from my childhood that connected me to my Mexican culture was the *paleta*, a Mexican popsicle made of fruit and sometimes ice cream. These *paletas* were directly connected to my mom's home state of Michoacán, and the popsicles are commonly called *La Michoacana*, the same way people call tissues Kleenex. These frozen treats are not just popsicles. Immigrants feel a nostalgia for their homeland of Mexico, and to enjoy a popsicle whose label features any version of a Michoacana girl logo or the name brings a cultural connection. My story is that on our trips to visit family in Mexico, the first thing we did when we got off the plane was go get a *paleta*—to have a taste of our homeland.

Now there are *paletas* being sold with the Michoacana name at Costco by a company that is not based in Mexico. But having the Michoacana name on the label provides the nostalgia that customers want, a link to their Mexican culture, something that would not exist if the product was just called a popsicle. As I researched the many companies that have produced *paletas*, I found out that my grandfather, who had a ranch and sold dairy, was connected to the Andrade family, who produce *paletas*. My cousin Raul Oseguera, who is also the proud owner of many *paleterias* in Mexico, connected me to Giselle Arbaca Andrade of the family-owned *paletas* company La Michoacana.

Case study: *Paletas* and La Michoacana

Popularity created imitation

Paletas were so popular that many independent ice cream parlors used the name Michoacana and a variation on the original logo of the girl used by the Andrade family. This is an example of a brand that got diluted, as there was no copyright protection on the logo. It is now known as an orphaned brand, owned by none and loved by all.

YOUR INSIGHT Is there a way you can protect your logo or your product?

Differentiate your product in a crowded market

When I asked Giselle Arbaca Andrade how her family company stands out in a crowded market, she responded, "Quality." They use only the best milk and fresh fruits to create a product with a high quality they hope their customers can taste, and this is their way to encourage brand loyalty. They also decided to not grow their company too big, because they want to maintain that high quality as a family-owned and -operated brand.

YOUR INSIGHT What are the differentiating features of your brand, and how can you stand out?

Uncover more about your roots

Early on, being Mexican American was not an identity that always filled me with pride, due to so many experiences of racial stereotyping. Traveling to Mexico City in my twenties was a turning point for me, and it was there that I learned to be proud of my Mexican heritage. I saw great cultural pride, high-achievers, and Mexican entrepreneurs. Now, I make regular trips to Mexico to get in touch with my cultural roots. Most recently, on a vacation in Tulum, I met a local family (not related to me) who welcomed me into their home and lovingly shared a meal with me, as well as their spirituality. Learning how different Mexican people live well and with such joy helps me have pride in calling myself Mexican American.

A friend introduced me to an amazing woman whom I interviewed: Sarah Culberson, who discovered she is a princess from Sierra Leone when she traced the roots of her Black birth father. She was adopted by white American parents, and as a child she felt she didn't fit in her family or community as a multiracial girl with a "huge Afro." Even though she had many accomplishments as a varsity basketball player and had earned a full scholarship to college, there were many internal challenges she needed to face. Sarah's research into her birth father led to finding community in Sierra Leone. That experience led Sarah to start a nonprofit, Sierra Leone Rising, to support community building in Sierra Leone, and her story is now being developed as a movie project.

Wisdom quotes from Princess Sarah Culberson, cofounder of Sierra Leone Rising, author, public speaker, humanitarian, philanthropist, and actor

Finding your personal mission
"It wasn't until I started to get older that I started to appreciate all the parts of who I am, so I could actually be [here] for others, which is what I feel like I'm here to do: to work with students, to work with young people, to empower them to do work in the world, to do work in Sierra Leone, to help with clean drinking water for wells. It was a great wake-up call for me."

YOUR INSIGHT Are there internal questions you need to answer about your identity? Any cultural challenges you want to make peace with? Perhaps there is a role that you are especially able to play for your community. Are you uniquely suited to connect the dots and solve a problem?

Write out your dreams and find your support

"What are you, what are your dreams? Are you writing them out? Write out everything you want. And think of action steps to take in each of those areas. Start sharing it with people who support you and your community... It really takes a team... Being a leader is really standing in your power and having incredible people around you to support you, and you support them back."

YOUR INSIGHT Have you written out your dreams? Look for people who are supportive and find a way to get their help. Perhaps you need a weekly meeting with a friend to help you think through your project. Ask around until you find your support team.

Tap into your imagination

What other things from your childhood create nostalgia for you? Putting on sunscreen from Banana Boat or even just the scent of it reminds me of my childhood summers, swim lessons, and vacation. I think of the train sets and miniature towns I built. Imagination is key to innovation and developing your dream business or career.

A company that has focused on creating toys that encourage imagination is Melissa & Doug. They have even partnered with the American Academy of Pediatrics to champion open-ended play, as well as establishing other partnerships to promote their mission.

Case study: Melissa & Doug, toy company

A strong mission statement

"Our mission is to provide a launch pad to ignite imagination and a sense of wonder in all children so they can discover themselves, their passions, and their purpose."

YOUR INSIGHT Study Melissa & Doug's website. Notice how their story and mission statement are communicated everywhere. The founders have photos of themselves with sock puppets, being playful. Do you have a website or social media platform that has your mission imprinted as well as this company?

What's your passion?

"It's through play that kids discover interests, passions, and talents. We want our kids to be happy and, ideally, building a career when they grow up that's true to their core selves. Figuring out who they truly are and what they love to do begins with play."

YOUR INSIGHT If you're not clear on the passion that helps drive your purpose, find a way to play and discover your old interests or maybe a new interest. Take a class, buy some art supplies, or join a recreational sports team to see what gives you your playtime. If you are clear on your purpose, find a new way to play and discover a new layer of that purpose.

Reflect on this chapter by doing the following exercises, designed to help you find your story, passions, and purpose.

EXERCISES

- What childhood memories or toys do you remember fondly?

- What things give your friends a sense of nostalgia or that childlike playfulness?

- What do your kids or your friends' kids play with? Are there new toys you want to learn more about? Are there old toys that remind you of your childhood?

- What is play for you? Draw, scribble, mold with clay, plant or arrange some flowers, play your favorite sport—see what comes up when you focus on this question. How do you harness this passion and play to your life, your job, your career path? See what fun things can support you in a fulfilling career path.

- Draw a timeline of your life and your most powerful memories or achievements. See how this can inform your story.

2

BE BOLD AND DIFFERENT

He couldn't remember my name,
but he found me on the
Internet as the singing realtor.

What's wrong with being different?

GROWING UP, I was always the odd man out. The big glasses, the acne, being short, being artsy. You know the type—and maybe it even describes you too? Even though I had taken soccer and swim lessons to make friends, I never seemed to fit in and I was bullied often. It wasn't easy to have friends. Because I wanted to blend in so badly, I wanted to change my last name so it might sound Italian instead of Mexican. Growing out of that awkward phase took a lot of work. It so happened that my talent for singing got me a record contract at 14 and took me on a path of training in the music industry.

My music managers taught me a lot personally and put me in a variety of classes. Hip-hop classes, working out, and singing lessons all gave me ways to feel more confident in myself. There were very few young Spanish-language singers at that time, and I was hoping to be the next Ricky Martin, to perform in both English and Spanish. My Spanish-speaking skills weren't so great, but when I sang, my Spanish sounded perfect. No other kid at school was running around to extra classes the way I was. When I performed concerts at a mall or local venue, I started to see my potential and gained confidence. I was a split personality: I was proud to sing in Spanish, but I still wasn't proud of being Mexican in a white-dominated school. But I loved my Mexican culture when I spent time with my family and my dad pulled out the karaoke machine and sang iconic Latin songs on the weekends.

I didn't have the words for it as a kid, but I was navigating different worlds. For those of us who are minorities or underrepresented, it is daily work to be code-switching from our own culture in order to blend in with the mainstream culture. I had a hard time embracing being different from the mainstream. Being bold and different is a lesson I wish I had been able to learn earlier, so I am sharing it with you here to propel you to your success.

This chapter celebrates trailblazers who took bold risks and dared to be different.

Face your fears

In order to have courage, you need to have fear. Courage is acting in the face of fear. A lot of us push away the fear, hoping it will disappear. You can never push it away. That is suppressing the fear, but it's still there.

When I performed as a young singer, my biggest fear was that the microphone would not work. It was a tough lesson to see the microphone fail 50 percent of the time. Eventually, I just learned to laugh it off.

Fears are so many, and you can end up collecting them—from fear of not being able to grow your business to fear of not finding that true love, of losing a loved one, of not being good enough, not being pretty enough, not being rich... and the list goes on. It's the collection of fears that holds you back from being your best self.

It was amazing how many times the microphone failed to work for my performances, but I just had to keep getting up onstage, and the experience taught me to let go of that fear. So what if you fumble? Pick yourself back up and keep going on your journey. Make a list of your fears and see how you can take small actions to face them. This is how you start to be bold.

Embrace your differences

While I didn't know I was gay until much later in my teens, I knew I was different. Later, as I came out of the closet as an adult, I realized that it made such a difference to see a gay Latino in the media. Wilson Cruz played an openly gay teen in the 1990s TV show *My So-Called Life*. Cruz was the first openly gay actor to play an openly gay leading character in an American television series. His media representation made it possible for me to learn to be proud of my difference. Now he is the first gay character on *Star Trek: Discovery*.

Wisdom quotes from Wilson Cruz, actor and LGBTQ advocate

Celebrate your differences

"Today you can turn on almost any television show and see a member of the LGBTQ community depicted and that didn't just happen. That happened because there were people who risked their lives and their livelihoods in order to tell those stories. And so now, really what the next step and the next level that we need to reach is allowing LGBTQ filmmakers to be behind the camera, writing those stories, directing those stories, producing those stories, and telling our own stories."

YOUR INSIGHT Is there a way for you to take a bold risk and represent your differences so you can help represent and reach your community?

Find your niche

"I thought that being Latino and being gay was going to hold me back and what ended up happening was, there was a void for a voice to speak to those issues of representation to those communities and my job was to identify that void and fill it. And to recognize that I had the ability to speak to those issues in a way that would be useful."

YOUR INSIGHT What can you uniquely speak about? Which communities do you want to represent?

Dare to create your own opportunities

"The truth was it was 1997, and I was too ahead of the world and the culture of the time. I needed to be patient and be present as things began to change and also be a part of that change. Part of the reason I took the job at GLAAD is because I and people like me weren't getting the kinds of roles that we should've been getting. So when I wasn't working I had the opportunity with GLAAD to go and speak to studio executives and network executives and lobby for more representation of people like me. I wasn't going to wait around for someone else to make those jobs available. I had to go and have those conversations for myself to create my own opportunities and to create opportunities for people like me."

YOUR INSIGHT What is a job you might be interested in that doesn't exist yet? How can you create new opportunities for yourself or your community?

Embracing all of you

Since being a creative artist like a music producer is not such an obvious path as getting a job at an accounting firm, these creatives really need to broadcast their brand for their work to reach an audience. My friend Mark Batson is a multitalented, Multi-Platinum, Grammy Award–winning music producer, musician, and composer who works with musicians from a variety of genres, including Eminem, Alicia Keys, Beyoncé, LeAnn Rimes, and Anthony Hamilton. He is a classically trained pianist from Brooklyn, and as a child he performed in Carnegie Hall and at the Brooklyn Academy of Music. He studied jazz piano at Howard University and is also a former pianist for the Smithsonian Institution's Program in African American Culture. He is also a composer for hit films such as *Miami Vice, American Hustle*, and *Triple 9*. His new age album created in 2020 to counter negativity, *I Want to See You Shining*, ranked number one on iTunes charts.

I asked Mark about how he works with so many different types of artists and how he manages to keep his own brand.

Wisdom quote from Mark Batson, music producer

What am I representing?
"There was so much heavyweight [news] on TV, watching people die, it was over the top. I started to make recordings to boost my confidence, to erase those negative images... Whatever you are representing, your motive, make sure you are so proud of it, it represents the best part of yourself, what you want for other people, or a need that other people want from you. Every single person has something dynamic; find that individual thing, or three to five individual things, and get really focused on those. Build your brand on that so that your purpose is reflecting who you really are, so you can reach the zone and keep putting out more product under that brand. That brand is representing the entirety of who you are."

YOUR INSIGHT Is your brand representing all of you? If not, how can you expand your brand to showcase your best three to five qualities?

It's about the journey

Soccer is such a big part of Mexican culture. My mom put me in soccer when I was a kid and I learned about playing on a team at a young age. I was not the star athlete, but I learned the discipline of drills and team sports. The journey of being on the soccer team helped shape my character.

Megan Rapinoe, a leader and pioneer among women's athletes as US women's soccer player and World Cup champion, does not shy away from controversy. Her values drive her leadership style and her brand. In addition to her excellence as a professional athlete, she's been outspoken about racial justice, LGBTQ rights, and gender pay equity. She talks about her boldness and operating as your authentic self. Taking risks as an athlete or as a person means risking failure, and she talks about how it's about the journey.

Wisdom quote from Megan Rapinoe, professional athlete and LGBTQ advocate

It's not about the winning

"I've lost a lot in my career. I've won a lot in my career. You kind of take it sort of all with the good. And I think particularly having the success that I've had in my career, I realize it's really not all about that. It's not about the winning. Oftentimes you win these games and you're like OK. Well then what? It really kind of is about the process and the journey and the people you're with and getting better every day and I feel like you just kind of take it with a grain of salt."

YOUR INSIGHT Think about risks you've taken and what you get out of the journey regardless of winning. What have you gained in the process?

Erase the negative self-talk

The pressure to assimilate in school and even in college was intense. It went beyond the negative self-talk I experienced when I wanted to tell people I was Italian instead of Mexican. I wanted to change my last name. I wore contacts that changed my eye color to green. I wanted to look like people who had money and were successful, and they were white, so I wanted to hide my Mexican-ness.

My music managers taught me to give myself pep talks when I looked in the mirror. Little did I know that my later mentors would teach me something similar. Affirmations, visualizations, and positive self-talk have helped me conquer what some call the "monkey mind" or the "chatterbox" of negative self-talk. The brain tends towards the negative, the reptilian brain that stops us from taking risks as a survival mechanism. Listening to coaches and motivational speakers is one way I push out the negative self-talk and stay positive.

Wisdom quote from Trevor Moawad, CEO of Moawad Consulting Group and coach to elite athletes

Quit saying negative things that you don't want

"Think more about the things you can stop doing right now—today. Think about putting a muzzle on negative expression for the next twenty-four hours. Negative thoughts can cross your mind. They will. But for one full day forbid yourself from verbalizing them. Witness the difference that makes in your relationships, your mental state, your outcomes. You'll be amazed."

YOUR INSIGHT Do you complain? Will you challenge yourself to do a detox from complaining for seven days in a row? Mark it in your calendar. If you mess up, start your seven days over again.

If you can detox from complaining, you will notice that negative thoughts will be less dominant in your mind.

Be proud of being different

Being a celebrity or artist in the public eye carries with it a lot of pressure to fit in and leaves one vulnerable to all kinds of criticism. A pop icon who has shown her strength despite being criticized for her race, her weight, and her sexuality is Lizzo, best known for her album *Cuz I Love You*. She has presented her body to stand up for what can be beautiful. Her confidence comes through in her song lyrics where she commands attention to her queen persona. She discusses freely in interviews about her point of view on body politics. Her brand of being bold and taking on controversies is what keeps her in the public eye and builds her a loyal audience.

Wisdom quote from Lizzo, singer, rapper, and songwriter

Change the terms of the game

"Girls with back fat, girls with bellies that hang, girls with thighs that aren't separated, that overlap. Girls with stretch marks. You know, girls who are in the 18-plus club... I think it's lazy for me to just say I'm body positive at this point. It's easy. I would like to be body-normative. I want to normalize my body. And not just be like, 'Ooh, look at this cool movement. Being fat is body positive.' No, being fat is normal. I think now, I owe it to the people who started this to not just stop here... We have to make people uncomfortable again, so that we can continue to change. Change is always uncomfortable, right?"

> **YOUR INSIGHT** Are there terms you want to redefine? Are there terms you can coin that distinguish your brand (and your views) from others' brands?

Find your niche

When I first started my real estate work, I specifically chose to focus on residential properties instead of commercial properties. Buying a home is an important landmark in someone's personal life, whether they just got married, need a bigger house for their growing family, or have to sell a family home because someone has passed. I wanted to make a positive impact in people's memories of their important life moments.

Now to get more personal. With my humble beginnings, our family trip to Las Vegas in 1999 made a big impression on me. We did not have money to go to shows, so we spent time walking from one hotel to another, sightseeing. That is when I fell in love with design. I connected to the gold and opulence of Caesars Palace. And I wanted to replicate the painted blue sky and clouds from their ceiling to my bedroom. Somehow, my parents helped me with my vision.

Instead of spending on movies and kids' stuff, I saved my money to buy home decor from the discount stores for my bedroom design. I managed to have over 15 gold and silver pillows on my bed, wooden columns with fabric drapings, and Italian gold curtains with tassels on my window. You could say I was ahead of my time. My room was the 3-D version of a vision board. When I look back, it seems inevitable that I would work in real estate.

More emotionally speaking, a home means so much to me. I had a falling-out with my parents when I came out to them about being gay, and for a time I did not feel welcome to stay at their place. For a few weeks during our discord, I lived out of my car and stayed at a friend's house. To have a place to go home to, where you feel safe and welcomed, is so important. These personal experiences led me to initially specialize in residential real estate, because I am so passionate about helping someone find the right home for their life.

When my friend introduced me to the financial advisor Humble Lukanga, I saw that we both came from humble beginnings, and I was so impressed with his personal story. He found a way to make a big impact with his financial career by finding his niche.

Case study: Humble Lukanga, wealth manager for professional athletes

Humble Lukanga grew up in Uganda amid genocide and starvation, escaping with family at age 11 to come to the United States under political asylum. Coming from Third World poverty and witnessing how professional football players went broke after retirement sparked his interest in serving as a financial advisor to this niche market of professional athletes. He is one of the top business and wealth managers, representing the biggest names in sports, entertainment, and business. He represents athletes who play for the Los Angeles Lakers and Hollywood stars like Issa Rae, and who he calls "mavericks and renegades, dynamic thinkers."

Celebrate your difference

"I want a young kid in Compton who's going to school and thinking about business to say, 'Oh my God, I can have that life?' They can look at my journey and say, 'If Humble can go through all that, I can make it too.'"

YOUR INSIGHT Is there something in your life that is bold and can serve as an example for your clients or for young people?

Sometimes it is as simple as sharing on social media with the hashtag that helps you connect with people. For example, if I post a photo of me at an LGBTQ community event, I get young gay men who look up to me as a mentor. Remember something from your past that shows your strength. I give myself the pep talk: "You've got this. What's the worst thing that can happen?"

Another colleague describes how important it is to find your niche. Liz Marie is a branding expert who specializes in serving small businesses and has a community outreach program that offers scholarships to women- or minority-owned businesses. She is dynamic, with her urban vibe and tattoos, and comes from a family where her mom is a schoolteacher and her dad a musician. She chose not to go into a music career, but her mission is to serve those who are creative and different.

Wisdom quotes from Liz Marie, brand strategist

Remember your essence

"There are all of these external socialization forces of other people's ideas that are obscuring [your essence]. It's all noise that blocks away and makes it harder to remember who you are. It's a process of chipping away at that and getting down to the root, kind of like a diamond in the rough. I think that's a huge parallel with branding... It's a process of remembering and getting down to the pure essence of what that is."

YOUR INSIGHT Take a moment to block out the noise. Close your eyes and take 10 deep belly breaths. Uncover the root essence of who you are.

Really figure out your audience

"To really know your audience, who are you serving? It is just as important to know who you are not serving."

YOUR INSIGHT Let's clarify: Who are you not serving? Who is naturally drawn to you that you might not notice is your audience?

Respond to the following exercises to help yourself discover how you can be bolder and celebrate what makes you different.

EXERCISE

- Draw a Venn diagram of your interests. These are your natural communities. After you draw your diagram, make a list of associations or groups where you can make personal connections to build your advocates and audience.

- Are there family pressures for you to do certain things with your life, your career?

- If there were no limitations of money or social pressure, what jobs or career choices would you pursue?

- What type of people are you easily drawn to?

- What type of people are drawn to you?

- How do you want to be remembered?

- Are there opportunities you are scared of taking? Why? How can you be courageous in the face of fear?

- How can you develop a support system to help yourself dare to be different?

3

AUTHENTICITY

If you're trying to be authentic,
you're doing it wrong.

Rejection as protection

WHEN MY record deal fell apart during my teen years, I felt rejected by the music industry and fell into a deep depression. These are the negative thoughts that plagued me: I felt my life was over. I felt I wasn't good enough; I wasn't a good singer. I thought music was my career plan and when that plan fell apart, I was so disappointed and sat in a lot of self-pity. I used to think to myself, "Now what? This was my purpose."

Looking back, I can see that the rejection was a good thing in my life. It's possible it pushed me to do other things and discover new opportunities. Even if the music career had worked out for me, I might have been too young and vulnerable to handle the success. I might have ended up dead from a drug overdose in the wake of all the intense pressure that has affected other young musicians. Or I might have let success go to my head and become a nasty person from the unhealthy attention I would have enjoyed as a celebrity. Because of all the insecurities I had, I might have stayed in the closet and not become my authentic self and instead become a very angry and unsatisfied person. I did not have the protection or skills to handle what a successful music career would have brought to me as a young public figure.

Knowing what I know now—how insecure I was, that I have an addictive personality, that I wanted attention for the wrong reasons—I recognize there is a large possibility I would not be here today to fulfill my bigger purpose. That rejection was a gift. The universe protected me from early self-destruction.

When the accounting firm laid me off in my early 20s, that rejection could have ushered in a devastating depression as well. Every time I got rejected or had a major setback, I could have been stuck in the dumps and taken it personally. But being laid off turned out to be another gift, because it prevented me from following the wrong path. The universe was telling me to take a right instead of a left. A rejection is a helpful push in the right direction. It is important to look at any big "no" as a message, a lesson, directing your spiritual purpose in a different way.

> **YOUR INSIGHT** What rejections have you had that created new possibilities? Imagine what could have happened if you'd had the opportunity to go the other way.

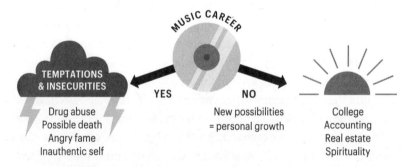

Fill out the graphic below with your own rejections and possibilities:

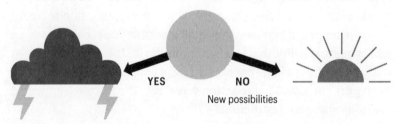

Being honest with myself

When I was recovering from a relationship breakup, some of the words my ex had said to me ran on repeat in my head. Was it true that I didn't love myself enough?

Throughout most of my real estate career up until recently, I was very disciplined about my work schedule during the week and then I would be a social butterfly on the weekend. It was my effort to be popular and feel important. That lifestyle had its aftereffects. On the weekend I would often be hungover, which affected how I spent time with my family. I was tired and lay on the couch, not participating in the family activities. My sister pulled me aside to tell me, "Don't bother coming if you can't be here and present." So I shifted my social functions to Friday nights only, so I wouldn't be desperately fatigued on Sundays with my family. I started to realize that I was abusing my body and that my brain wasn't as clear as it could be. I had so many ambitions, and here I was causing myself to operate at less than optimal capacity. Being clouded in my thinking for several days after the late nights was not helping me reach my goals. My purpose was not being served. I wanted to do more in life, and I needed to be more alive. Looking back, I understand that I had an addictive personality. Even then I saw the danger signs, and knew it was better to stop the excessive lifestyle before it got worse. I could compare myself to others and the way they overindulged, and rated myself a 2 out of 5, but I knew I was still toxifying my body and hurting my ability to achieve my dreams.

I decided to quit drinking and to surround myself with others who also did not drink. Making this choice to be sober was my choice to be more present. But I had already made this decision many times. For five or six years, I would stop for a couple of months and then I would get back into drinking, and it was worse than before.

There's a lot of pressure when you're in a society where drinking is normalized or it's part of a luxurious experience at a party. Alcohol was slowly destroying my life.

On the outside, I wasn't at the bottom; I was still making money and winning awards. But on the inside, I felt lonely, depressed, anxious, and unworthy of my success. I had a bleak sense of my future. Frequently, in my dreams, I was lying on a piece of driftwood in the middle of the ocean, and I was alone, there was no one and nothing around me. I would wake up feeling so alone, even though I have an amazing family and so many friends. One bout of drinking on Friday night would cause me to not feel normal or clear or present until Tuesday. It seemed I was broken.

On New Year's Day 2020, I felt lost and took myself for a walk down to the Santa Monica beach. I saw a road, a path made in the sand by some unusual tire marks, which I followed to the end of the beach. There, I saw some people meditating. Even though I wasn't planning to meditate, seeing these people inspired me to sit down and do my own meditation.

It was at this moment, on the beach, that I realized I needed help to get sober, because I hadn't been able to do it on my own. Usually, when I want something, I know how to get it. For example, if I wanted to win a sales award at work, I knew how many phone calls to make and the sales numbers to reach. I was usually good at reaching goals. But somehow I hadn't succeeded in achieving my goal of cleaning up my alcohol habit. During that meditation, I got really honest with myself. That moment at the beach, I finally decided to get help. I had tried to be sober on my own and it didn't stick. When I started meditating, it was cloudy, but when I finished meditating, it was sunny and my friend had called to ask if I needed help. I saw the significance of that meditation and the parting of the clouds, and agreed to go to a support group meeting that day.

Being sober has made me feel more powerful than ever. I don't need the "fake friends" who were only there for the party. I can use my time more wisely and curate my experiences to be more meaningful. And the bonus reward I wasn't expecting was that I got into the best shape of my life! And my allergies went away. My physical health confirmed that I had made the right choice. It feels so good to be the best version of me. After just one year of sobriety, my parents told me they almost didn't recognize me. I can see they are so proud of the better version of me.

Work on yourself, and know when you need help. Before my sobriety, I was sometimes egotistical to the point where I thought I didn't need anyone. But I had to surrender to the fact that I couldn't do this all by myself anymore. I felt so defeated—I was embarrassed when I showed up to my first support group meeting. I was shaking in my seat. A colleague remembers seeing me holding my head, slumped forward with my elbows on my knees. On my first sobriety anniversary, she said how proud she was to see my transformation.

Before becoming sober, I wasn't grateful. I just wanted more notoriety. I was negative. When people asked me how I was doing, I would talk about how hard I was working and complain about things that weren't going my way. During my first year of sobriety, in 2020, I could reflect on the fact that the old version of me would have been self-absorbed and not have cared about the global crisis. Now, as a sober and higher-functioning version of me, I help spread the good mood and positive attitude to help uplift other people. When people ask me how I am doing now, I share my gratitude.

Finding support

In my new sobriety, I was invited to a networking lunch with my friend Marina. She had previously been sober in a support group, but she looked as if she was having trouble that day. In our casual conversation, I said I didn't drink anymore, and she asked if I was part of a group. I shared how I'd had the most amazing year and how healthy I'd been and all the things I'd accomplished. She told me that when she had a support group and was sober, she also had the best year of her life. She confessed that she lost her sobriety because she had a peer group who didn't support her sobriety. Because I was sharing my gratitude and success, Marina asked to join me at one of my meetings. She has been sober and happier ever since. I am glad that my success inspired someone else to get back on her path to happiness.

Even before becoming sober, I had a good morning routine in place, did all the things such as meditation, visualization, and working out. Now, this new lifestyle choice was the missing link that let me feel my best. Without that mental cloudiness and physical lethargy, I can fully be the best person I was meant to be. Even without my drinking buddies dominating my weekends, I still laugh a lot and I'm a fun person. I now do things with clarity and full presence. And I have reshaped my environment to surround myself with more genuine friends who have healthier lifestyles.

These genuine friends contribute to my life in different ways. They are my informal "board of directors." They comprise different support groups: health friends, sobriety group, business networking friends, social friends. They all give me something, a different perspective on the world. For example, the business networking friends give me leadership opportunities and share their strategies for work success. My sobriety group provides a space where I can get over my embarrassment at my mistakes and focus on my gratitude. My health friends share my enthusiasm for eating well and working out. It is helpful to know I am not alone and have people in my life who want to help me be my best self.

YOUR INSIGHT

- Do you have any bad habits or poor lifestyle choices that you might consider changing? How are these parts of your life limiting you, or interfering with your achievement of your goals? If you want to make a change, how can you get the support or change your environment so that you can succeed in making the change? Have you tried and failed to make the change before? What did you do before, and what can you do differently this time to be more successful?

- Who would be your ideal "board of directors"? If you don't have those friends or support groups now, who can you ask to help you find them?

Looking at opposites

I love my sister and I see how different she and I are. When we were kids, we were such a team. When I accidentally set the closet on fire, she helped me put it out and cover my tracks so that I wouldn't get in so much trouble with our parents. (Yes, I was playing with fire and it got out of control, so I tried to hide it in the closet.) She has always been a good teammate for me, being honest with me and supporting me. However, her choices have not been focused on career ambitions. Her purpose is very different from mine: she wants to be the best mom and partner in her family life. I see her differences and her talents, and her wonderful life, and I am proud to be her brother.

Part of being authentic is looking at my preferences. I have made a choice to focus on career goals, so there are parts of me in family life that I haven't developed and could learn about from my sister and other family-oriented friends. Do I want to improve my work–life balance? How can I better relate to clients and people who are not like me?

By looking at opposites, I can learn to embrace the wholeness of who I am, and the wholeness of human nature. This effort helps me be more compassionate and a more relatable person, which in turn helps me be of better service to my clients and my audience. If I show dislike towards a particular aspect, that would reflect an underlying bias that is off-putting to potential friends and clients. Doing this work of noticing and accepting opposites is important for the personal growth of self-love, self-acceptance. For my community, it is a way to be genuinely compassionate and accepting of others and to invite others to see me as likable and respected.

The same way plants need to drop their dead leaves to make space for new leaves, and things need to decay in order to create fertilizer for new growth, opposites are how Mother Nature balances life and an ecosystem. Authenticity is looking at the light and dark sides of the color spectrum and seeing how we can have a truer vision of what is really there.

YOUR INSIGHT

- What pains do you avoid? What pleasures do you chase? Can you accept and balance those both?

- What needs to be destroyed or let go of in order for you to create the life you want? Is there "busywork" that you can delegate to someone else so you can focus on growth? Are there hobbies or friends you may have outgrown, and that do not help to create a supportive environment?

- Are there certain things that you habitually think are true? Write them down, and now write down the opposite. Can the "antitheses" be true as well?

- What is the opposite of your brand? Can exploring this opposite be helpful in your message?

Get real with your strengths and weaknesses

If you have a business consultant with an MBA background come look at your business, they are likely to start off with a SWOT analysis. This is an important tool for business planning, especially if you are considering a new project or direction. This is something you can start to do for yourself, beginning with your own self-awareness. And if you need help getting real with your strengths and weaknesses, you can ask your friends to give you some honest feedback with a survey or even just a more in-depth conversation. If you are a solopreneur—someone who has set up and runs your own business—you can do two analyses of 1) your personality and 2) how you approach your business, and you will likely discover the two are the same. If you have a staff to support your business, you will consider the strengths and weaknesses of your team members in addition to your own (see chapter 7, "Building a Team, Expanding Your Brand").

You can do this exercise for yourself as an individual and also for your business to be aware of where you stand in your business environment. SWOT is an abbreviation for the internal aspects of Strengths and Weaknesses (S and W) and the external position of the business environment in terms of Opportunities and Threats (O and T). This analysis can help you discover new strategies based on your Strengths and Opportunities that will help you overcome your Weaknesses and Threats. This is a good exercise in which to involve your team members, friends, customers, and community members, so that you can get an in-depth view from all perspectives.

Here is an example of a SWOT analysis for a performing artist/ musician launching her second album. Indie musicians are usually solopreneurs, so her personality is leading her business and her branding. She is a 20-something singer-songwriter, an indie artist without a big budget, who plays acoustic guitar and violin with a sweet folky voice.

INTERNAL ANALYSIS	EXTERNAL/ENVIRONMENT
Financial resources (funding, sources of income, and investment opportunities)	Market trends (new products, technology advancements, and shifts in audience needs)
Physical resources (location, facilities, and equipment)	Economic trends (local, national, and international financial trends)
Human resources (employees, volunteers, and target audiences)	Funding (donations, grants, and other sources)
Access to natural resources, trademarks, patents, and copyrights	Demographics
Current processes (employee programs, department hierarchies, and software systems)	Relationships with suppliers and partners
	Political, environmental, and economic regulations

S · STRENGTHS	**O · OPPORTUNITIES**
Has a good network to help host paying private house concerts	Music videos are catching new fans and exposure
Has a devoted fan base	Digital downloads are growing
Has good artistic music videos	Demographics of new fans are young
Loves to collaborate with other musicians	Direct marketing efforts garner new fans
Has a strong community of other musicians to do joint concerts	

W · WEAKNESSES	**T · THREATS**
Doesn't have own recording studio	Political environment is not leaning towards easy listening folk music
Doesn't know how to sound-engineer recordings	Other artists are also competing with Kickstarter campaigns to fund their albums
Not technically adept at explaining to engineers what sound she wants	Economic downturn means people are more selective with their donations
Tends to have songs with a similar vibe	

Based on this SWOT analysis, a business consultant might recommend these strategies for this musician:

1 Invest in your own recording studio so that recordings can be done more quickly and at lower cost. Or, find a fellow musician who is able to provide a home recording studio at a low cost or in exchange for your musical skills, such as guitar or violin accompaniment.

2 Partner with a sound engineer or music producer who is also a musician. Since you are good with collaboration, this weakness can be overcome if you can tap into the strength of your community.

3 Produce music videos that contrast with the vibe of the folky sound of the music. Cowrite a few songs with edgier songwriters so there is a variety of songs on the new album. Stay true to your brand, but also use collaboration to expand on your variety of themes.

4 Focus on promoting a few songs that are more current and relevant so that fans can buy into "feel-good" songs on the album.

This indie artist has a low budget, so for her to expand, we need to help her identify her nonmonetary resources. Her social network and community are fantastic resources. Depending on who this artist meets, one person could really change her situation. If she meets a patron who can single-handedly finance her album, then she could still use her community resources to get her songs to sound more distinct and competitive in the market.

YOUR INSIGHT

- Do a SWOT analysis on your personal skill sets. Discover your strengths and find out if you might need further training to help overcome any skills gaps. Pay attention to the items in your W and T categories, and use this insight as you go through the next chapter, "Invest in Yourself."

- Do a SWOT analysis for your business. Ask friends and/or your team to join you in this exercise.

- What recommendations can you (and your team) come up with to overcome your Weaknesses and Threats?

Businesses with a mission

Your brand can be distinguished with a unique mission. My brand stands to elevate and reach the luxury market. I stand for high quality, great design, and attention to details.

My mission is to give someone a warm, welcoming home. This means I help people find their home; happiness is my brand.

I look to other business and community leaders as my inspiration. There are only a few selected ones we can quickly discuss in this book. On my *Brand With Podcast*, you will hear about more businesses I admire and meet more inspirational leaders.

Case study: Cisco Home

Your values and community impact

I love great design and I want to support businesses in my Latino community. Cisco Home was originally established in South Central Los Angeles. Its founder, Cisco Pinedo, came from a small Mexican village, and his upbringing had given him a deep sense of community and connection. Through his business, not only does he have elegant design, but he also integrates environmental sustainability into every piece. As a pioneer, Cisco Home is a founding member of the Sustainable Furnishings Council. At the foundation of his business, Cisco also builds community by training people from underserved communities to have job skills and partners with community groups to reach the next generation. Cisco Home has chosen to be a leader exemplifying its values through its business practices, and that makes it a distinct brand.

You can start with something that takes little time, such as making donations to community groups that represent your values.

Or, you can get your company or business to provide mentors to encourage more underserved youth to explore their career choices. If you don't have the necessary influence at work, perhaps you can ask a colleague who is more senior to help you make the community impact you would like to stand for.

YOUR INSIGHT What values do you stand for? Are there associations you can join? How can you integrate your values more into your work or schedule? Can you volunteer, be a board member, or ask your company or business to donate to community groups that make the impact you want?

If you want inspiration through video, there is a miniseries on Netflix portraying the life of Madam C.J. Walker that has me excited: *Self Made*, starring Octavia Spencer. This story of a washerwoman who rises from poverty to become the first female self-made millionaire in the United States, building a successful beauty business, reminds me that anything is possible. I want you to have that feeling too, that your potential is unlimited.

Case study: Madam C.J. Walker, entrepreneur, activist, and philanthropist

Where is your determination?
Born Sarah Breedlove, one of six children, her older siblings were slaves and she was the first of her family to be born into freedom. Orphaned at the age of seven, she was quickly cast into work as a child domestic servant and had only three months of formal education during Sunday school literacy lessons. As a laundress,

she was determined to make enough money to give her daughter a formal education.

YOUR INSIGHT What fuels your determination? Do you have goals that drive you? If you haven't found what drives you, do you have friends who are very determined? Remember, your informal "board of directors" can support you in your goals!

Organizing and training others

At the height of her career, Madam C.J. Walker employed several thousand women as sales agents for her beauty products. She harnessed the power of branding by packaging her products with her image, representing her products for Black women. Not only did she advertise, she personally traveled to promote her products and focused on training her sales teams to budget and become financially independent. She held an annual conference, and organized her sales agents into state and local clubs.

YOUR INSIGHT If you are new to your career, what organizations can you join where you can get training and get noticed? If you are running your own business, how can you organize and train others in a way that upgrades and promotes your brand?

Philanthropy

As Madam C.J. Walker grew her wealth, she made a great community impact with her generous donations. She also became an active public speaker and helped raise funds in the community with many key local groups. She designed her home, Villa Lewaro, to be a community gathering place and to host public events.

> **YOUR INSIGHT** Is there something you can leverage from your skills or assets to support your efforts in making a community impact? Do you belong to an association to which you can lend your space for gatherings? Are you good at public speaking, so you can support your values at community events?

Lead with a mission

At any point in your career, you can become a public speaker or podcaster or write about the values or issues you care about. While it is helpful if you have more power or wealth, I am inspired by people who have overcome great challenges and have the boldness to speak out and become advocates.

> ## Case study: Lizzie Velásquez, motivational speaker
>
> ### Transforming a weakness or threat into your brand
> Lizzie Velásquez was born with a rare disease that caused physical conditions, which resulted in her being subjected to bullying during her childhood. So many of us get bullied for our physical traits. I was skinny with big glasses, and that was enough for me to get bullied. Velásquez bravely chose to be a public speaker and post YouTube videos. She overcame being called the "World's Ugliest Woman" by becoming a successful motivational speaker, a social media figure speaking against bullying, and an author with works published in English and Spanish. She has been featured in a documentary, *A Brave Heart* (2015), and starred in her own TV series.

> YOUR INSIGHT Is there something in your Weaknesses or Threats categories that you can transform into your unique inspirational brand? Is there something that other people have tried to shame you for that you can overcome in order to stand proud?

EXERCISES

- Listen to Darryll Stinson's TEDx Talk: "Overcoming Rejection: When People Hurt You and Life Isn't Fair."

- Name the top two or three "rejections" that have impacted you the most. How did they hurt you? In what form—insecurities, self-doubt, negative messages? Are there lessons you can learn from those incidents? How did each incident change your course, and what would have happened if you had stayed where you were? Follow-up: Name three incidents where you had to say no to a person or project because it wasn't a match. How were you better off for saying no? What was a better match for you in your purpose?

- Take a project you are planning to launch or a current project. Do a SWOT analysis and see what you can do to minimize the challenges you find in the areas of W (Weaknesses) and T (Threats). Ask for help from friends and colleagues if you need feedback on your analysis.

- What symbols might represent your brand? They could be animals, images, archetypes, characters from a myth or story, or philosophical words. How can you let concepts from your unconscious become more present in your consciousness so they can be expressed in your brand?

- Read and reflect on Robert Frost's poem "The Road Not Taken":

Two roads diverged in a yellow wood,
And sorry I could not travel both
And be one traveler, long I stood
And looked down one as far as I could
To where it bent in the undergrowth;

Then took the other, as just as fair,
And having perhaps the better claim,
Because it was grassy and wanted wear;
Though as for that the passing there
Had worn them really about the same,

And both that morning equally lay
In leaves no step had trodden black.
Oh, I kept the first for another day!
Yet knowing how way leads on to way,
I doubted if I should ever come back.

I shall be telling this with a sigh
Somewhere ages and ages hence:
Two roads diverged in a wood, and I—
I took the one less traveled by,
And that has made all the difference.

- Think of a few times in your life where you had two paths you could have taken. What would have happened had you taken the other path? What did you learn because you chose the path you did take? Compare and contrast the benefits of both, and the challenges of both.

- Are there choices you made because the alternative was scary or too different from your regular life? Can you say what reasons made you make one choice and reject the alternative?

- Take this fantasy ride: For each path not taken, identify what might have changed in your life had you taken it. For example, if you took a "safe" job, what would have happened if you had tried out your wildest idea of a job that you were really interested in?

4

INVEST IN YOURSELF

Invest in your mind, invest
in your health, invest in yourself,
and upgrade your life.

Reputation as a brand

MY MATERNAL grandfather, Max, was a hard worker, ambitious, and a true entrepreneur who built something out of nothing. As the father of 14 children, Max was able to grow his business from a dairy farm, expanding into the meat business. He grew from having one farm to four. My grandfather was one who invested in himself and, most importantly, in his reputation. He didn't call it his brand, but that's what it was.

People around town knew him as a man who played by the rules, a man who was honest and treated other people with respect. Everyone trusted him. Every deal was done with a simple handshake, no contracts. That is how much trust people had in his business agreements.

My grandfather had a special fondness for me. I was born in July, and by December I was speaking, which is unusual for a baby less than six months old. At that time I couldn't even walk yet, and my early talking surprised everyone in the family. My grandfather remarked, "My god, this kid's going to be something special. He has a lot to say." Soon, I was talking along with the commercials on TV. The family was amazed that I was also singing at an early age. I was in my crib and would sing along with soap opera theme songs on TV. As young as age three, I would come out from behind my parents' bedroom curtain and create a stage performance as a little singer.

When my grandfather passed, he left his Rolex watch to me. He chose me out of all his 14 children and dozens of grandchildren. That Rolex watch meant a lot to the whole family, and it meant a lot to me. My grandfather knew that watch was going to help someone open doors to grow entrepreneurial success, and he was not going to give it to someone who would just sit with it at home. It was his gift to me because he knew I had ambitions. It was a symbol of how my grandfather believed in my potential, and his blessing as a successful entrepreneur gave me a reminder that I had the strength to succeed and get through any challenges in my entrepreneurial path.

When I first started working, I wore my grandfather's watch proudly. It was the only thing of value that I had, and it was the first luxury watch that I owned. I was so proud it came from my grandfather, and it gave me confidence. Watches are an accessory I have. loved since I was a kid. Watches also represent time, and I care very much about time. At the beginning of my real estate career I would wear my very inexpensive suits and ties, but when I looked at my left wrist and saw that special watch, it would remind me where I came from. It brought my grandfather to mind, a man who would invest in himself and his company, for growth and expansion. It reminded me of the importance of investing in yourself and investing in your brand.

When I was struggling at the beginning of my real estate career, I could have pawned the watch, but I would rather wear a hole in my old shoes and borrow against my retirement savings than part with that watch. A new Rolex might cost about $15,000 and I have never wanted to get my grandfather's watch appraised because its value to me is priceless. Ultimately, that watch is not about the monetary value, but the sentimental value of what helped boost my confidence in my early entrepreneurial days. It is a symbol that people far richer than me noticed, and it showed that I cared to accessorize with something classy, expressing my brand as classy. That watch helped me be seen and respected past my inexpensive suits. It allowed me to look put together and confident. You could say it was my lucky rabbit's foot, and it brought me more than $15,000 in business deals in my early career. When I was eventually able to buy my first luxury watch, I put my grandfather's watch in a fireproof safe to protect it. One day, it will be passed on to the next young entrepreneur in my family, and I hope it will give them the confidence it gave me.

YOUR INSIGHT

Symbols: Do you have something symbolic that gives you strength and confidence? For some people, it might be a particular pair of shoes, a jacket, or a lucky charm.

Words: Can you recall a story or moment where someone else believed in you? Maybe it was something someone said about your qualities or your brand?

Rituals: Do you have rituals that make you feel more confident? For instance, doing a "power pose" for two minutes, as described in a TED Talk by Amy Cuddy, has helped job interviewees and test takers reduce their cortisol levels and feel more confident. Some people jump up and down or run to get the anxiety or stress energy out of their body. Other people do breathing exercises to get their body together and focus on being present. Can you do your ritual(s) before a big presentation or meeting and see a difference?

Write down the answers to these questions to support you on the days you need a boost, a reminder to keep investing in yourself.

Create a morning routine

I had a roommate and friend who was unusually accomplished, managing two successful businesses. He got up at 4 a.m. and accomplished so much by 9 a.m., more than most people do in a day. I was amazed by his hard work and results, and so I tried out his routine. Since then, I have been getting up at 4 a.m. to do my morning routine. Rising early makes room for the "me time" that helps jumpstart good energy and organizing before my business day begins with phone calls and clients.

Before I had my roommate's example, it wasn't obvious to me that I needed more time in the morning to get in my workout, journaling, meditation, etc. I used to get up around 7 a.m., which I thought was okay for me. But if I had stayed up late the previous night, my morning routine would get thrown off. It takes a while to figure out how much time you might need to do your meditation and the other things that help you set up your day. Some people might need a full hour for meditation, while others require only 20 minutes. I listen to podcasts while I do my run, and that helps achieve two objectives: learning and exercising. I reflect on what I hear in the podcasts. I have a paper journal and I also save my thoughts on voice memos on my phone, to help me remember later. Sometimes I get good ideas while exercising, and I step aside to talk to my phone. Some people are good with a 20-minute yoga workout; I need more time for my exercise routine, which involves a weights workout and cardio. Notice how you need to portion your time in the morning. See what you can combine if you need to manage your time better.

Highly accomplished people, including star athletes, actors, comedians, and CEOs, have mentioned how important meditation is to them and have advocated for their companies or teams to make time for meditation. The list of meditators includes Oprah Winfrey, Tony

Robbins, Hugh Jackman, Kristen Bell, Arianna Huffington, and Jeff Weiner. If you look up accomplished people you admire, you will notice how often they mention meditation as a key ingredient of their success. LeBron James is known to use the NBA game's time-out to meditate and optimize his performance. That time-out is only 75 seconds! It just shows that you don't need a long time to do a "reset" on yourself to help you focus and let go of stress.

Personally, meditation reminds me of what brings me joy and a sense of gratitude. It helps me remember the important things when there are so many things to do. Some people call it focus, centering, or grounding. I may get different results each time I meditate, but I stick to it because I know that people I admire say how much meditation means to them.

Meditation seems to lead to a lot of confusion or difficulty for some people because it is not as obvious as lifting weights or putting on your sneakers for a run. Decide you want to try it and know you will find a way that works for you. There is no *one way* to meditate; there are so many techniques. Some people call it mindfulness, others do breathing exercises. Some people start with a meditation app on their phone or listen to a guided meditation on YouTube. Others shut down their technology and sit quietly. A friend of mine who doesn't like to "sit" does breathing exercises while she is taking a shower or washing dishes, and she calls this an "active meditation." There are resources like meditation retreats that you can do online to jump-start your practice if you want an in-depth experience. Or if you need a daily practice, find classes or recordings that suit your schedule. As long as you are turning inwards and feel an awareness of your breathing, that mindfulness breathing is the start of your meditation.

Wisdom quotes from Aaron Keith, CEO and founder, Buildify Systems

Aaron's journey as an entrepreneur started at 19 when he launched his first business. His company, Buildify Systems, trains hundreds of entrepreneurs with its business education and coaching programs. For his success, he credits his own investment in learning and having incredible coaches and mentors. Today, he is a highly sought-after business coach, and he has personally mentored me in my personal and business goals.

Train your brain and how you think

"My business coach taught me [that] how you train your brain and how you think has a huge impact on the actions you take. It's not just business. He was a huge proponent that it's also personal growth. You have to grow as a human if your business is going to grow. So it was a mix of business development and personal development, and that combination for me was just the most exciting thing I've ever seen."

YOUR INSIGHT What do you need to grow personally in order to help your business grow? Is it a quality such as confidence, empathy, forgiveness, or discipline?

Design your morning routine

"I believe that morning routines are critical for all people. Sit, reflect, journal, read... any kind of morning routine is powerful. I think everyone has to find the ingredients that make up their morning routine."

YOUR INSIGHT What ingredients do you need to set up for a morning routine that supports your business?

Sleep hygiene

How you prepare for sleep affects how well you sleep so that you can start your day the way you want. Since I plan to get up at 4 a.m., I need to plan to go to sleep around 9 p.m. Everyone has an optimum amount of sleep they need. If I stay out later for social functions and have a later dinner, I am going to need to adjust my expectations for the next morning so I can perform at my best.

If I need to decompress from a high-stress day, I might have to go for an extra run to clear my head or journal to help myself focus on my priorities and gratitude. I use my foam roller every night to stretch out. I joke with my friends that "you shouldn't go to bed dirty!" Taking a bath is a good way to wash away my day as a reset and to relax the muscles in preparation for sleep. Many experts say that watching TV before bed is not good for the eyes and melatonin. A friend says she likes to watch relaxing footage of animals or ocean creatures before bed. Sometimes I need to "zone out" with an old favorite show I have watched hundreds of times, like an episode of *The Golden Girls*, as a way to turn off my brain. Some people like to read a book or write in their journal. Figure out what works for you.

> YOUR INSIGHT What do you need for your sleep hygiene? Is there something that hasn't worked for your morning routine, such as journaling, that might work better as part of your evening routine?

Stress management

To be a good leader or manager of your business, you need to prioritize and have good stress management. If I don't manage my stress, it will affect my sleep and attitude. When things are bothering me and I need extra help, I call a friend from my inner circle, my personal "board of directors," to ask for their insights.

I also make sure to take vacations regularly to unplug and gain perspective. Recently, I went with a best friend to Big Bear, driving distance away from Los Angeles, for a cabin getaway and to be in nature. I wasn't planning on going to a cabin; it was my friend Imene who initiated that. Being open to the unexpected gave me a fun three-day weekend that provided a much-needed recharge. It was an important experience that was an investment in our friendship and also a great stress reducer. We laughed hard, I got to be silly with the way I cooked breakfast, and my friend pointed out some things about me that I wasn't aware of. Being around her, a trusted person from my inner circle, felt so good. If all you have is a weekend, find a way to shake up the routine of your regular life. Even if you can't get away, you can do something intensive for a few days that is an investment in stress management—a stay-at-home meditation retreat, perhaps, or you could help a friend landscape their yard.

I also took a big week-long trip with a different friend to Cancún, where I met a Mayan family and had a chance to reconnect with my Mexican roots. A longer trip really gives me some space to get a different perspective on my life and my business goals. While travel is my preferred stress reduction strategy, it might be something different for you. Some people sign up for a week-long music camp. Others join a community group to rebuild homes as community service.

Other things I do to manage stress are:

- revisit my gratitude list
- organize my closet
- rewatch an old favorite TV show
- play with my nephew
- spend time with my family
- sing, or record a song as a voice memo to send a friend

One mindfulness teacher says that stress management can be different for men and women. While everyone benefits from breathing exercises and meditation, men may be more drawn to exercise because it helps boost their testosterone levels. Women who exercise will also get the boost of testosterone, but they might get better stress relief from bonding with friends or window-shopping, activities that help boost their estrogen and progesterone hormones. Find out what works for you. What your friends need for their stress management might be different for you. Doing something nice for others is a way to share joy and have it reflected back to you. I love to record a voicemail with a personalized "Happy Birthday" for my friends and special clients. Not only is it doing something nice for someone to show I'm thinking of them, but it also enhances my brand. And I also get great joy from that activity, which is a bonus point for my stress management.

> **YOUR INSIGHT** What helps you manage your stress on a daily basis? How often do you need a short getaway for stress management and good mental health? How often do you need a longer retreat or getaway? Make a wish list of things you would like to have for your stress management, share it with your friends, and perhaps someone will invite you to their activity and help you get your recharge.

Learn new habits and get things accomplished

I'm driven by my own internal expectations and yet I find it helpful to have coaches for different areas of my life. I have a coach for real estate, who has industry-specific expertise to help me grow, and I have a business coach to help me grow in my general business skills.

I also have a life coach who helps me balance my daily work and life schedule. While I am self-motivated, it helps to have external support to keep me on track. If individual coaching is not within your budget, there are accountability groups, or you can have a buddy system with a friend who has similar goals.

One way to learn new habits is to take the Four Tendencies quiz by self-improvement author Gretchen Rubin. The way we respond to outer and inner expectations determines our "Tendency" type—whether we fit more into the category of Upholder, Questioner, Obliger, or Rebel.

- **Upholders** like to have rules and know what should be done.
- **Questioners** want to know the science and the "why" behind a practice.
- **Obligers** need accountability: they need a workout buddy or a group exercise class.
- **Rebels** need the freedom to do it their way: don't tell them what to do!

I am generally an Upholder; I like to have discipline and routines. I am self-motivated to eat healthy and go to the gym, because those are habits I have already put into my lifestyle. When it comes to learning new habits or doing new things, I am more of an Obliger. Some of us benefit from a "drill sergeant" approach, while others rebel at being told what to do. By taking this quiz, you will gain a better understanding of what encourages you to learn a new habit and what is not helpful. With this self-awareness, you can choose what kind of course or coach best supports your new skills and habits.

Consistency matters

Studies show that a daily habit is easier to stick to than something that isn't daily. If you're trying to figure out a routine, do something that can help you stick to it. Use a paper calendar on your bulletin board with the new habit you want to accomplish for your routine, and reward yourself with a star or sticker. Even though we have technology, there is something to be said for a physical reminder of our goals and accomplishments. These reward systems from our elementary school teachers help our inner child decide we're having fun and make us want to stick to our new routine.

It is said that if you do something every day for 21 days, you have created a new habit. And if you can get to three months, it becomes part of your lifestyle, something you don't have to think about anymore. Find something you already do daily, like brushing your teeth or taking a shower. Pair your new habit, such as stretching or meditating, with your existing habit, and that's how you can get your new habit to stick more easily! If your new habit doesn't feel desirable, find a way to make it more fun. Most people need a buddy to help them stick to something like a new exercise routine, so if your goal is to have better hiking endurance, do it with a friend. Or find a class to help you get your groove.

Since I want to upgrade my public speaking abilities in Spanish, I have joined a Toastmasters group for Spanish speakers, and as a bonus I have met new colleagues and increased my social network. A voice acting teacher uses tools from the Internet to generate word lists on specific topics to build vocabulary and a random sentence generator so students can practice enunciating different words and sentences. You don't need to become a voice actor to take a voice acting class. Shake it up to use a bigger vocabulary. Becoming a better public speaker is important for communicating your brand. These are different ways to find resources to improve your public speaking skills. Committing to a course or a weekly group is a way to build your skills consistently.

There is a common problem with being a beginner: it is so easy to quit because we don't feel confident about our abilities or we judge the quality of our efforts. Radio personality Ira Glass has coined the idea of the "taste gap." You have great taste, so you have the ambition to create something great. As a result, if you take up watercolor painting as your creative outlet and your first paintings don't look as good as you imagined, it is easy to become frustrated and want to quit. As a beginner, your early works are not going to be very good, and because you have taste, you know your work is not up to your own standards. And this is where most people quit. For your entrepreneurial success, you have to be willing to risk failure and not being good at something when you're in the beginning stages. The goal of the beginner is to create a volume of work or variations of your product, practice your sales pitch on different people hundreds of times, or try your ways of meditating in different scenarios. If you stick to it and find ways to refine your methods, you will find your success.

> **YOUR INSIGHT** List the new habits you want to learn and see what support you need to be successful. Can you carve out 21 days to focus on one new thing? It is hard to launch a lot of things at the same time. Prioritize what is an easy and important win for you.

Wisdom quote from Mark Batson, music producer
You'll find an outline of Mark Batson's life and career in chapter 2.

How to be good at your passion
"Continuously do it every day. If you want to be great at something, just do it every day. Consistency beats out a lot. Record constantly. When you can, just create, then present. Consistently just create. That's who the race goes to. It goes to the person who is more driven by the creative process, who's going to do the work, and enjoys the work... Understand that some of those first recordings might not be great, but it just leads to the fact that the 100th recording could be great... You have to stay consistent, working."

YOUR INSIGHT If you don't have a consistent daily habit of keeping a journal or creating, how can you structure a practice into your day so you can "do the work" of creating something every day? Is it a matter of setting up a separate space for your music or creativity?

Being consistent is so helpful in keeping me strong in my mental health and focus. But sometimes life stressors and events happen to knock you off your routine. And when that happens to me, I feel that I am off track. Once you're off track, it is easy to want to stray. Advice from various coaches says to just pick it up and get started again.

YOUR INSIGHT When you get off track with a routine, what small thing can you do to get back on track?

Confront any weaknesses or shame

In chapter 3, "Authenticity," I talked about my journey of sobriety. I had tried to get sober on my own, and that was my weakness. I needed a support group to help me be my optimal self. If you need to reread that chapter to do a SWOT assessment to figure out your weaknesses, you can find exercises there.

Part of my weakness was wrapped up in shame. I previously did not get help because I had shame about my weakness. It took a friend reaching out to me, someone whom I perceived as accepting and supportive, for me to say I needed help. In many self-help books they talk about your "shadow self," the things you don't like about yourself. If you can face your dark side and love all the parts of you in order to feel more complete about yourself, you can build your confidence and be more successful. If you have any shame energy around, that weakens your presentation of yourself and your brand. Now that I have confronted something that was previously deeply shameful, I am more confident than ever.

As a child and young adult, when I was around wealthier kids at school, I had shame that my father was not a wealthy businessman and that their families made more money. My dad was and still is a hard-working school janitor who also worked in his off-hours as a house painter. I always knew that I got my strong work ethic from both my father and my mother. However, my perspective has shifted. Now, as I have matured, I am so proud of him. I have rewritten that old, unfavorable story to recognize that my father provided a safe and clean environment for schoolchildren and shared his warm, friendly personality with kids who needed an adult to talk to. I have let go of the old shame of my immature self and now share the pride my father has in his work.

Bad posture is an example of a seemingly small weakness that can have a big impact on your confidence. A friend has a habit of slouching because he was the awkward tall kid growing up and he tried to blend in with his shorter friends to make them feel more comfortable. Even though his habit comes from good intentions, he has to remember to straighten up when he does presentations. He knows he has this weakness, and instead of worrying about it looking unusual, he happily shows off his physical therapy shoulder harness, shaped like the straps of a backpack, to remind him to straighten his posture. He shared his difficulty with his colleagues in meetings in a lighthearted way and gained more confidence. He is a tall guy and that is part of his brand, and his humor about his weakness has become a charming aspect.

Some people feel bad about their math or reading ability, which may have been affected by dyslexia or perhaps a lack of compatible teachers. If you might have an undiagnosed learning disability, it is good to get some tools to improve your performance and confidence. Some people are terrible at learning names or other memory challenges, and there are courses that give you strategies for overcoming these weaknesses. Always be learning so you can overcome your challenges and shame. Your entrepreneurial success depends on your best confident self.

YOUR INSIGHT

- What personal weaknesses do you want to work on? If you need help prioritizing, ask a trusted friend or coach. What do you need to learn to support your business?

- What areas do you have shame about? Can you rewrite your shame as if you are the director of your life story? So many versions of the same movie can be made. Can you remake that story of shame into something you can be proud of? It is similar to finding the silver lining in a struggle.

Wisdom quotes from Ricky Singh, international fashion executive

Ricky Singh is an executive leader managing the international fashion business Cactus, and a member of my friend Anisha Manchanda's family. As the founders of Cactus are aging, he is learning every aspect of operations and marketing and travels globally to manage their vendors and client relations.

Believe in yourself. Confidence matters.

"The reason why you're an entrepreneur is because you are a leader. You have people working for you, [so] be decisive. That's the most important thing: believe in what you are saying. If you are wishy-washy, and you are not confident in what you're about to say, no one's going to follow you; no one's going to believe what you're saying."

YOUR INSIGHT Do you believe what you're saying? Is your confidence communicated?

You are selling yourself

"[When] sitting with a client... honestly, just be yourself. If you ever try to sell the product, 9 out of 10 times the sale will not go through. Because 10 out of 10 times, you're not actually selling the product, you are selling yourself. So if you sit in front of a client and you approach them from a friendship point of view, with honesty, whether they like your product or not, they have to buy *you*, and if they buy you, your product can change. And they'll buy whatever you put in front of them the next time, [even if] they didn't like this product this time."

YOUR INSIGHT How do others describe your personality? How do you bond with your clients? If you need personal examples, find someone in your network who excels in sales and figure out the ingredients of their confidence and likability.

Be open

Being open to learning new skills and asking for help is key to my personal and business growth. When I started my business and was going to networking events five days a week, I met my friend Vincent Jones, who was so great at connecting with people. If he saw someone who didn't have anyone to talk to at an event, he would take the extra steps to introduce them to someone in his circle. He was so helpful in introducing me to anyone I wanted to meet, and I could see he was truly an active listener, caring about understanding and remembering conversations. His social interaction represents his personal brand of kindness, humility, and care. He is a good example of how to better connect with people at networking events, which can be intimidating or awkward. Vincent is someone you could look to model yourself on, as you can see he is open and always learning.

Wisdom quote from Vincent Jones, social entrepreneur, change agent, and CEO of Citizen Jones Travel

After 25 distinguished years as an accomplished professional in politics, philanthropy, and social entrepreneurship, Vincent turned his passion for travel into a business.

Always learn new skills

"I taught myself how to build websites. When I was in high school, I would go to the local community college to take classes. I've watched weird documentaries about random things [to learn new skills]. Always be learning. You never really know when that skill set or idea will mean something. If you have an idea, write it down, and build mood boards. Put things in a file, or a Pinterest board, or whatever technology you want. You might not do the idea at that time, but you might do it 5 or 10 years later. If you don't write it down now, you might lose that creative spark."

YOUR INSIGHT What idea can you write down and expand on? If there are opportunities for this, can you find the team that can help you expand your idea and possibly take it to execution?

Can you bring up an idea you had years ago? Can you refresh and expand on that idea so you can remember it in detail, in case you want it for later?

EXERCISES

- Are there aspects of your brand that need help? What can you do to build support in that area? For example, if you need help with public speaking, what can you do to support the part of you that needs to broadcast your brand? You could hire a public speaking coach, join a practice group for public speaking like Toastmasters, watch YouTube videos, or take an acting class. Who in your team can you practice your new skills with?

- Meditate: Figure out when you can meditate. Get inspired by your walks, while exercising, drawing, or watching the sunrise. You can even meditate when you take a shower or bath.

- Vision board exercise: If you've made a vision board of what you would like to be doing over the next few years, what courses or learning do you need to get there? If you haven't already made a vision board, get started! This can be something you cut and paste in a book or on a poster board, or you can do it online on Pinterest.

- What continuing education subjects or skills or topics would you like to study? No limitations on cost—put it on the list. Even if you can't do it now, you never know when there might be promotions coming or a new friend who can help you learn!

- Healthy habits: Read one book a month to instigate new ideas. If you're already reading that much, add another book to your stack.

- Put together a mastermind group with other professionals whom you respect and can learn from on a topic that you need support on. You can be a complete beginner or at an intermediate level. Try to surround yourself with at least one peer who is more advanced in this mastermind group.

- Revisit your weaknesses. If math is a weakness, do you need to take a course like Accounting 101 to learn the vocabulary you need to communicate better with your CFO or accountant? If you don't have a good design vocabulary, perhaps a course in color theory can help you have better conversations with your creatives.

5

PERSONALIZING VIDEO

Only you can be you, and
that's your superpower.

Representation matters

GROWING UP IN Los Angeles back in the '80s, I rarely saw people on television who looked like me. Hispanic, Mexican, and Latino faces were rare in the media. People I saw most were singers like Jennifer Lopez and Ricky Martin. I understood that being on television showed you had power. Since I wanted to be someone important and have influence, I pursued a singing career—so I could get on television.

I remember a pioneer whom my mom would get excited about seeing. María Elena Salinas was the first female Hispanic TV news anchor on the new Spanish-language channel Univision. Her presence and confidence inspired our family. Little did I know, until I later did some research on her, that she struggled with shyness.

When I was training with my music producers as a teen, I worried about my looks, felt shy, and did not feel comfortable performing in front of a camera. With the hard work and practice of going to dance and singing classes, and from positive affirmations, I built up the confidence to overcome my shyness. These days, when I produce videos for my social media or other branding projects, I receive so many compliments about how my videos are well made and how I look so confident in them. Everyone has their journey to feeling confident in front of the camera. This chapter is just the beginning of you getting your videos personalized to reflect you and your brand. If you want a deep dive and to get your videos produced, I invite you to take a look at my course Brand with Video, where you'll receive exercises designed to get you feeling and looking professional with video.

While video marketing is a mainstream concept today, it wasn't always so affordable to produce branded content. Many professionals used to rely heavily on cost-effective print and email marketing methods to gain market traction. One day, I decided to take a chance and start my own video marketing campaign with a camcorder, before cell phone cameras became high quality and mainstream.

When I made that first video in 2011, about the reduction in mortgage interest rates, I was so shy that I didn't want anyone to watch and judge me, so I shot it on the rooftop of my apartment building so there wouldn't be any passersby. In the background were the Hollywood Hills, which provided a great backdrop for my brand with Coldwell Banker. When I pressed the red Record button, I was sweating. Recording a three-minute video took me an hour and a half, and it felt like forever. I was so frustrated with myself, and my nerves got more wrecked by my negative self-talk. To top it off, I noticed a woman a few buildings away watching from her balcony. I was waiting for her to go away before shooting more footage. Between the internal and external pressures, that first video was a painful hurdle. However, when it was done, I got so much positive feedback from colleagues and friends that the final product was worth it. I was a pioneer in making video marketing a pillar of my brand. I, as a first-year realtor, had found a way to stand out among more experienced colleagues.

If I could communicate my brand's mission through a video, this would allow me to appeal to a variety of clientele and differentiate myself from my competition. Sure enough, with time, consistency, and creativity, I was able to expand my brand footprint. Over the last 10 years I have received local community recognition and been invited to speak at conferences and give interviews. I have become an example for other realtors. As a result of my video production, my business sales, my confidence, and my audience grew exponentially. Now, colleagues whom I have not met in person refer clients from everywhere in the United States because they have seen my videos. I even get client referrals from London and Brazil.

Presenting my brand over video didn't come without its own personal hiccups. I had to overcome a great deal of stress and fear to get to where I am, especially while getting used to being in front of the camera. Many people are afraid of being broadcast. We have this perception that thousands, if not millions, from all over the world are going to see our videos and criticize in the comment section. Although some people are not as accustomed to making short-form content on TikTok or starting their own YouTube channels as most of today's teens, personal insecurities around being in front of the camera have always been somewhat the same. Younger entrepreneurs reach out to me for advice because they have seen my videos. I am glad to serve as a role model.

In childhood, I had a high-pitched voice. All kids have high-pitched voices when they're young, but mine was *extra* squeaky. For years I was incredibly self-conscious about my voice and I would actively try to make it sound deeper. It wasn't until after puberty that I finally felt comfortable with my voice. Unfortunately, I allowed my childhood insecurities to bother me for years and years after the fact. Every time I heard my voice on the answering machine, this sinking feeling would pop into my head. It affected my confidence and self-esteem to the point that I wouldn't speak up in class or go out to introduce myself to people. I allowed my insecurity about my voice to take over my life. It wasn't until many years later that I started to record voice memos in college and began to connect with and appreciate my voice in all its quirkiness. It took hearing myself over and over again to reconnect with a part of me that I should have cherished all along. Now I love my voice. It defines me. It's what sets me apart and makes me special. I hope that with this chapter we can dive into the healthy mindsets that will help you build a positive and worthwhile brand that can rise to new levels through incorporating video production into your marketing matrix. And once you accomplish that, no one can take that power away from you.

What you do before you record, to be mentally prepared and have the right attitude when planning out your videos, is just as important as the actual recording. Confidence is key. Whether it's the script content, the location, or the props, going into the filming process with passion will drive your project. Deep down, you have to know that what you're creating is going to be of value for someone, even if it's just one person. Being able to compel and excite even a single person should be enough to inspire you to make your ideas a reality. But it's not just about you, it's about what you're there to deliver to your audience. Once you change your headspace, setting up your personalized video branding will come with ease. It's all about taking a chance at the cost of failure. Being completely honest with yourself is what will lead you to growth as an entrepreneur. The true value will come from expressing your authentic self.

When people watch a video, they learn about your brand in two ways. First and foremost, the brand can be seen as the actual product or service that is being offered through the video. And second, the brand is who you are, and how well you are providing that product or service to the viewer. When people watch your videos, they will be looking at the personality, expertise, and energy you have in promoting and selling your brand. The product doesn't even really matter. What is crucial to keep in mind is that your content is a way to show your audience who *you* are, and *why* they should trust you. The goal is to create an audience that looks at you as an expert in your line of business, even if you are still new. Through thoughtful, educational, and value-adding content, you can create a group of loyal followers who will support you in your business.

Mental mindset

What inspires me to get over my insecurities is that I want to reach more people and show them my personality. More people will see my videos than I can meet in person. Remembering the "why" or the goals I want to achieve helps me get through the challenges. In our own heads, being on camera is like being onstage with tons of people watching us. Camera fright is just like stage fright.

Even though I have made hundreds of videos, when I develop a new video, I sometimes need to remind myself of the 3 Bs that I recommend to my Brand with Video students:

1 Be coachable.
2 Be open-minded.
3 Be comfortable being uncomfortable.

It's very important to have the right mindset when planning out your content and before you record your videos. A positive emotional vibe is needed for your video to work. If there are insecurities, get help from people who have the skills to support you. You need to be excited about every aspect of the video, from content to location to props.

In my experience, these are the top three reasons that most people are afraid to make videos:

1 They don't like how they look onscreen.
2 They don't like how they sound.

3   Just plain fear. They're afraid of doing it wrong, afraid of being rejected, afraid of what other people might think. They fear they are only wasting time.

Many people are afraid of the camera. While some social media influencers may seem very comfortable on camera, that ease comes from the sheer volume of video they create. We all experience similar concerns and insecurities. The difference is that they push past their doubts, they test what works best, and they try again. They push through the fear and anxiety. Be sure to do the exercises at the end of this chapter to help you push through your own fear factors. Look at the case study of a professional journalist below and see how she had to work through her own fears.

Case study: María Elena Salinas, journalist, producer, and philanthropist

María Elena Salinas, former anchor of the highly rated *Noticiero Univision*, is a trailblazer who became the first female TV anchor on American Spanish-language media in 1981 and was also the longest-running female anchor in the United States. Coming from radio, she learned to thrive in the TV profession, where she had no prior experience. For more than three decades Salinas interviewed more world leaders and political figures than any other female journalist, winning Emmy Awards and other recognition for her work. Salinas has been honored by *Hispanic* magazine as one of the "100 Most Influential Hispanics" in the United States. In her philanthropic work, Salinas is active with women's organizations and Latino/Hispanic organizations. She is a former vice president and founding member of the National Association of Hispanic Journalists.

Ignore the negative voices and take the chance

"I needed to overcome some obstacles. Being a woman in a man's world, especially being a woman in Spanish-language media. Not allowing the fear of the unknown to stop me... There is no worse obstacle than the one that we have in our head, you know that voice that tells you: 'you can't. You're not good enough, you're not ready for this, you might fail.'... We have the choice to either listen to it and deprive ourselves from what could have been or ignore it and take the chance."

YOUR INSIGHT Face your fears. What are the negative voices in your head saying? Write down the negative statements and then cross them out. Now write down compliments you have received. Write each compliment 10 times and read it out loud 10 times. Put your most empowering compliments in a spot where you will see them every day.

Raise your hand and stand out

"I was kind of shy. My first two weeks on my TV job... I got laryngitis, you know the medical term for being petrified. I went back to school... and watched other reporters. I realized they were asking the same questions I had wanted to ask. I started raising my hand and I have not stopped asking questions since... Don't be a conformist and don't allow yourself to be mediocre."

YOUR INSIGHT Observe your peers in your field. What are they doing that you would like to be able to do? How can you differentiate yourself and excel?

Use your passion to drive your career

"I felt an incredible responsibility... There was a cultural and language divide that I felt that I could bridge... I became passionate about empowering the community that I was representing, that I was informing, that I was also a part of. That is what became a part of my life mission."

YOUR INSIGHT What is something that you can uniquely do for your community? How can you use your passion to help yourself overcome your fears or drive your career?

Practice makes better

Often, we are afraid to fail. With my background as a singer and the work ethic my mother instilled in me, I know that if I practice something, I'm bound to get better at it. If I want the first try to be perfect, I would stop myself from even starting. So often, we are trained to be perfect, but ultimately, you need to put in the time and you will see improvements.

One of my coaches said I needed to improve my vocabulary to sound more professional, and I could have let that comment knock me down. Instead, I saw it as an opportunity. I gave myself a 21-day challenge to focus on noticing my speech habits, and I was able to improve my vocabulary and confidence. As it turns out, I needed to take out some of the bad habits of the southern California culture; I used "like" and other colloquialisms too often. Once I paid attention to detoxing those filler words out of my speech and began to speak a little slower to give myself time to gather my thoughts, I quickly sounded more confident, even in the first week. And there were other habits I cleaned up. Sometimes I look up at the ceiling to find a thought, and I learned to keep my focus forward. And with the laptop camera,

I needed to position my computer better so I could make eye contact with my conference call audiences.

YOUR INSIGHT What speech habits do you have that you would like to "detox"? Are there other things you have received feedback on that you would like to improve? If you haven't received any feedback, who in your circle can give you some? If you don't have an expert or coach in your circle, you can join a public speaking group like Toastmasters to practice.

Wisdom quote from Janelle Monáe, singer, songwriter, and actor

It is now standard practice for musicians to make videos to go with their songs so that their music can get more attention. Janelle Monáe has been cutting-edge with her video production and the stories she tells. A recent song, "Turntables," came with multiple videos. She is not shy about sharing her unique point of view.

Perfection is often the enemy of greatness

"I want to be clear to young girls, I didn't have to change who I was to become a CoverGirl, I didn't have to become perfect because I've learned through my journey that perfection is often the enemy of greatness. Embrace what makes you unique, even if it makes others uncomfortable."

YOUR INSIGHT Maybe you're not comfortable with your brand or how you look on camera. What can you embrace that makes you unique, that you feel proud of? How can you expand on that uniqueness and take it further in your brand and your public persona?

Storytelling strategies

Being creative with video to tell a story is a way to connect with your audience. No one likes to be sold to. Think of your video efforts as educational, as a personal connection. If you have the resources or a contact that can help you craft an entertaining story, even better! My good friend David Beebe has turned his storytelling skills into a production company that creates "branded entertainment." In a few projects, he has featured travel locations and stunt actors to create an action short film featuring edgy lifestyle brands. People love to be entertained and escape into a fun story.

Wisdom quotes from David Beebe, brand storyteller and producer

David Beebe is an expert in branded entertainment, working as an executive producer with clients like Marriott Hotels and personalities like Arianna Huffington. He identifies marketing opportunities that bridge marketing and storytelling.

Engage with your audience

"Brands must stop interrupting what consumers are interested in and become what they are interested in. Marketing is like a first date: if all you do is talk about yourself, there won't be a second. If you want to be relevant, you need to start thinking like a media company and publisher, and add value to the consumer first."

YOUR INSIGHT Think about your target audience. How can you make content that they are interested in?

Look at soap operas as an example

"Back in 1956, when the soap operas *As the World Turns* and *The Edge of Night*, both produced by Procter & Gamble Productions, debuted as the first half-hour soap operas on the CBS television network... they were part of the story naturally. Win the hearts, minds, and wallets of consumers."

YOUR INSIGHT Is there branded entertainment, such as soap operas or short films, that you like? What elements would you like to use for your own videos?

Build relationships

"The relationships that you build now are going to help you later... You never know that one person you meet, how they're going to help you one day."

YOUR INSIGHT Do you have strong relationships with others who can promote you on their videos or be part of your videos? Think of what relationships you are missing and be on the lookout to meet those people or ask friends to introduce you to those types of people. For example, think of great camera techs or musicians whose songs you might want to feature in your videos, who would be great partners in making your productions more unique and personal.

Find your personal touch

"Always be learning and investing in yourself and not thinking that you know it all. What can you learn from other people? Whether it's in strategy and how you do something... someone's got their little personal touch that's going to make it different."

YOUR INSIGHT What is distinctly you? If you like art murals, you could produce your videos in front of art murals. If you like gardens, you could produce your videos in front of gardens. Whatever your personal touch is, people love to get to know you better, and it will help them trust you!

Advice to his younger self
"Get out of your own way. Typically, if you look at anything, you're going to be fearful of what other people think. What are you really afraid of?"

YOUR INSIGHT What beliefs or limitations get in your way? Ask a friend to hold you accountable as you try to stay out of your own way. If you need more help to be more uniquely you, please reread chapter 2, "Be Bold and Different."

Get helpful feedback on your videos

One of the biggest fears people have about posting videos is that someone will leave a negative comment. This *will* happen. As we all know, there are trolls out there just looking to cause trouble. Ultimately, it is a negative reflection on the commenter, not you. It used to bother me, but now I've gotten past it. I feel compassion for these people. It's not about YOU. If you need to build confidence before posting your video publicly, focus on getting positive reviews from your supportive circle first. You could even turn off the comments function on your YouTube channel if you want.

Focus on knowing that what you have to say is going to be of value for someone. Even if it's just one person, that will emphasize how important it is that you deliver the information. It's all about changing your headspace. It's all about personal growth and being complete with yourself, expressing your authentic self, and successfully creating a way to promote your business. Reread the chapter "Authenticity" (chapter 3) or "Be Bold and Different" (chapter 2) to help support your confidence. Over time, you will develop an ecosystem of people who will follow you, and that positivity will inspire you to keep creating more video content.

EXERCISES

• Watch some videos for inspirational coaching or videos from your industry. Watch these videos with a focus on identifying what it is that you like and would like to emulate in your own videos. Write down those qualities.

• Perform a fear analysis of why you are not doing videos regularly. Take a piece of paper and draw three lines to create four columns. In the first column, write one of your specific fears. In the second column, write *why* you feel that fear. In the third column, write what would happen if that fear actually came true. In the fourth column, write how likely it is that the fear will actually come true. If you still need help overcoming the fears on this worksheet, have a discussion with a friend or coach.

• Choose a pop culture event that excited you. This could be a movie, a song, a book, or a public figure's speech. Record a 30-second to two-minute review of the event.

• Record yourself on video, interacting with others (with permission). Take a moment to celebrate the things you do well in the video. Take inventory of the things you would like to improve upon.

- If you want help with your speaking or on-camera work, find yourself a public speaking coach or acting coach. You can take a group class or look for individual coaching—whatever suits your learning style and budget.

- Practice in front of friends you trust and get some constructive criticism.

- Be consistent with your video efforts if you want video to become a valuable branding tool.

6

SOCIAL MEDIA INFLUENCE

Every post is a way
to express your truth.

Social media as contact management

I T WAS through social media that I built my real estate career at the beginning, when I had no marketing budget. It provided free advertising and a large network to build, and all I had to do was put in sweat equity to create content so I could broadcast my brand to a large audience. I learned early on that social media is a branding tool whether or not you are intentional about it. So why not curate your content on social media and scale your marketing reach to a global level?

When I was in college, Facebook was more of a directory, a way to find the contact details of someone I wanted to date. In other words, it was an informal dating page. We treated our Facebook wall like a profile on Match.com. The poke function was used by someone who was interested in going out on a date. Somehow, I was unknowingly building a social network of college classmates during those early days of Facebook. Social media allowed me to quickly research someone's personality and interests. It became a powerful tool to grow a business network. These days, giving someone your Instagram handle is still a way of interesting a potential date, but it has so many other functions.

I want to use my social media to spread positivity. So I started a weekly resource on IG Live, *OK! Let's Talk*—a 30-minute interview show for a six-month run at the beginning of pandemic. I was getting phone calls from friends in the entertainment and restaurant industries who were looking for a way to be active and connect. They had questions about a career change and were looking for ideas about pivoting. I was reaching out to my network to ask about people who would give insightful interviews and improve my network. It felt good to offer a distraction, entertainment, and inspiration during a time of difficulty when people were dealing with the initial shock of the pandemic.

Social media has become such a huge and integral part of our daily lives. If you're not posting something yourself, you're commenting on or liking someone else's post. The closest thing to social media in my childhood years was trading yearly school pictures and writing sweet nothings on the back. I used to carry around all the photos and phone numbers of my entire class and share them with other friends. Now, with social media, the whole world is at your fingertips.

When I was starting my career in real estate, I saw the potential in using social media not only to advertise the homes I was selling but also to market myself. Before Instagram and YouTube, Facebook was a free way of advertising myself to my entire social circle. Before Facebook added a business component to its model, I was able to use this instead of spending money on expensive print advertising. I would post at least three to five times a week about real estate, and about what I was learning and doing. As soon as YouTube picked up more audience, I started my real estate series *Real Estate Minute*. This YouTube show was what put me on the map. I would cross-post my show across all the channels on Facebook, LinkedIn, and Instagram. I made sure there was consistency throughout all my posts, which meant I posted each item at the same time and on the same day. Social media helped me sell homes and build my brand. I was able to build a reputation as the local market expert at no charge. My social media is a way for people to research me anonymously, to validate a referral, before they decide to reach out to me.

Social media is also a way to stay connected with past clients on their life events, functioning as a contact management system. I organize my time to curate quality content. Be careful to not post too much, where people react to it as noise. The engagement feedback will help you figure out your rhythm and identify quality posts.

If you're an entrepreneur who is new to using social media for your business, start with searchable themes. Is it truly in line with your brand to post food photos even if food photos are popular? I try to make my social media presence more personal by responding to Instagram messages asking for advice with a personalized voice memo, something that has more presence than a quick text. I don't want anyone to feel ignored, especially since they had the courage to ask for help. Responding to comments and questions creates a conversation, and I want to be friendly and engaging. This is my stamp on my brand.

You never know who is watching. Your intention behind social media is important. Some people don't click Like or comment on posts, but they are still paying attention, maybe without you knowing. Social media is a way for me to leverage my time, to maintain my friendships, and to connect with more people than I could otherwise keep up with. I depended on that connection at the beginning of the pandemic when I opened up about feeling alone and shared that on Facebook. Friends whom I hadn't talked to since high school or other distant periods of my life showed kindness and support. Generally, I try to keep Facebook inspiring and fun to look at. Sometimes social media doesn't show my human vulnerability, and so this rare post stood out against my brand of positivity and engaged people in an unexpected way. This was an example of how authenticity and quality engagement is more powerful than wowing your audience or amassing a large number of followers.

Some public figures manage their own social media accounts as a way to stay accessible and communicate directly with their audience. I admire how Wilson Cruz is one to boldly share his point of view on social media and respond personally to comments.

Wisdom quotes from Wilson Cruz, actor and LGBTQ advocate

Connect directly with your audience

"Your audience wants to feel like they have a direct line to you and I like being accessible in that way. I could probably have a lot more followers if I did less controversial opinion-oriented postings, but that's not who I am. If you knew me on a personal level, these are conversations we would have, but I'm sharing them on social media. That's just who I am."

YOUR INSIGHT Do you want to manage your social media personally? If not, how do you want to direct your social media manager?

Speak on what is important to you

"My brand changes as I change and grow. Because I've been so clear about what is and isn't important to me, when people are looking to partner with someone on specific issues, I tend to come up. I think because I am so specific and I'm not just on social media to get more followers, that's why the exchange between me and my followers is more direct and meaningful."

YOUR INSIGHT Would you like to partner or collaborate on certain issues or topics? How would you like to position yourself as an expert or spokesperson?

Creating virtual relationships
and expanding your network

Not only have I been able to reach out to friends of friends through my social media contacts, my social media presence has allowed people to find me and become clients. When a colleague refers a potential client to me, the referral wants to see my personality and my brand. My *Real Estate Minute* videos are everywhere, showcasing my knowledge of a neighborhood, the Los Angeles lifestyle, and industry savvy. Most recently, a new real estate agent found me on social media and asked to use my video about the Pacific Palisades, a neighborhood she serves. I was happy to lend my resources to her and help her career as she was being creative in serving her clients with more neighborhood knowledge. We didn't have any connections in common, and it is exciting to me that my video had such a reach to help a new colleague. You never know when sharing resources might lead to more relationships and referrals and, ultimately, more business opportunities.

I posted a request on my social media looking for a videographer in Los Angeles. Everyone started putting names in the comments. Among a dozen referrals, Valentina Vee stood out as a creative, out-of-the-box thinker. She had a fantastic portfolio of work on her social media that impressed me. I could see that she had partnerships with big brands like Adobe and she has generated quality support on social media. Valentina is vulnerable and shares her emotional journey of success and challenges, and that makes her a three-dimensional person I can trust. She showcases the honesty and humanity of life, with all its ups and downs, and this makes her relatable. We became fast friends, and she is so productive with major projects—which is why I needed to share her wisdom with you.

Wisdom quotes from Valentina Vee, filmmaker

Valentina Vee is a filmmaker based in Los Angeles, with commercial clients and an Emmy-nominated docuseries. She was born in Kazakhstan and raised in Silicon Valley, and she went to the Design Media Arts and Film program at the University of California, Los Angeles. While at the university, she served as creative director of FPS Productions, UCLA's largest film society. Not only is she a great leader and a creative person, she is fearless in letting her personality shine through her work.

Use social media to find mentors and your career path

"Curate who you follow on Instagram... people that will give you ideas for your own creativity later down the line—and this is something you can foster in yourself... You need to have your heroes. You need to have your people who are maybe two or three steps ahead of you on your same journey. When you message them, you need to have a plan, you need to have a question, whether it's you're interviewing them to better yourself or you're asking them [for] advice... More likely than not, they'll respond. And in some cases, they'll go back and look at your profile... If it shows who you are, then they'll know you're legitimate."

YOUR INSIGHT Are you following your heroes or people more advanced in your field on social media? Do you have people you would like to ask for an informational interview? Make a list, reach out, and grow your network of mentors and peers!

Your social media reputation and partnerships

"You look at a lot of people who are working with these major brands on a high level as producers or directors. Even if they are on social media, they don't have much of a following, because it doesn't matter. You don't have to worry about followers, you don't have to worry about where you live, because by the time you're worth something, people will just fly you out. They'll care enough about what you have to say and your unique point of view that they'll just book you tickets to go where you need to go."

YOUR INSIGHT Social media contacts are about quality, not quantity. Are you too busy counting your followers? Who are the type of people you want to follow you? How are you commenting on or connecting with their social media accounts?

Use social media to extend your brand

Social media is another tool to extend my brand. I value being written up in traditional press such as *Forbes* and *Newsweek*, but my audience might not see that news without me sharing it on social media, where I can also broadcast my upcoming events and celebrate my wins and manage the timing of my accomplishments. Knowing that good news might get archived or crowded out on the original press or event websites, I can share my successes and message on my social media for as long as I want. My friend Phil Lobel, a leading PR expert who started his career in a time before social media, comments on how valuable social media is.

Wisdom quotes from Phil Lobel, owner and president of Lobeline Communications

Social media extends the shelf life of traditional media

"Social media has amplified traditional media. If a client has a story on *Good Morning America*, once upon a time the only people who saw that were people who recorded that on TV or were watching it in real time. And then its shelf time only existed just for that moment. But social media has amplified traditional media by giving it a shelf life that is ad infinitum. That is something that can be seen by millions in a country or around the globe."

YOUR INSIGHT How can you use social media to extend your message?

Manage your social media as an asset

"Social media today amplifies many times over what traditional media used to provide. If you're going for a brand identity, your brand can reach so many more people, so many eyeballs, because it can be shared. The downside is you have to be careful. The wrong message or wrong post can tank you just as fast as it can become an asset."

YOUR INSIGHT Do you have a system for quality control of your social media messaging?

EXERCISES

- Who do you admire on social media? What do they do that you want to imitate?

- What is the demographic on social media that is a segment of your larger audience?

- Create a marketing calendar so that you can maintain a consistent social media plan.

- What companies do you like on social media, and how can you use them as inspiration for yours?

- Stay away from all the "isms" (racism, sexism, classism, homophobic remarks, etc.). Remember, you want your social media to bring people together, not split them apart. Scan your old posts and see if you need to edit your page or repair any mistakes.

7

BUILDING A TEAM, EXPANDING YOUR BRAND

Talent wins games, but teamwork
and intelligence win championships.

MICHAEL JORDAN

Growing your team

IN ELEMENTARY SCHOOL, I was already making a great income selling chocolates, Power Rangers cards, and pretty much anything I could get my hands on. I knew that if I wanted to make even more money, I needed to split myself into five little pieces or… hire a team. I was able to recruit three other kids from the playground to help me sell my products: Joel, Melissa, and José. I could pay them either by splitting the profit 50/50 or by giving them some of the product to take home for themselves. As a child entrepreneur, I didn't really know about child labor laws. My main objective was to hire a team to expand my enterprising plans so I could make more money. I needed to trust each person and also find kids who could tap into new customers from different grades and different areas of the playground. We had very different personalities, but we shared similar values and, most importantly, we all had the drive to make more money for our own candy and toys.

As one person, you don't have all the skills you need to run a successful business. So you need to build a team, know what vendors or consultants to hire, and what staff you need.

First, if you haven't already taken some personality tests to get to know yourself better, it is important to identify your individual strengths and find where you need to fill gaps. In this chapter we have several types of assessments you can check out to see how they can help you know yourself and know what you need for your team. Second, you will want to have your prospective candidates or current colleagues take assessments so that you, as the leader, know how to manage your organization better. And lastly, I have interviewed two key mentors in my career who have built many organizations in their decades of work in real estate. While their industry specialty is real estate, their advice and insights are relevant to building a successful business in any industry.

Values

First, know your values and write them down. Then find the right questions to ask when you interview others so you can find people who share your values. This is the heart section of the chapter, following your gut. A good team has synergy, connection, and chemistry among its members.

Here are some examples of my values:

Honesty and integrity. Take responsibility for your life choices. Sooner or later, people will show you who they really are. How you do something is how you do everything. Ask about the "challenges" they have faced and how they overcame them. How they tell their story will show if they handled their challenges effectively or if they see themselves as a victim. Everyone has challenges to their character, and each person needs to take responsibility for their part in the situation.

When something goes wrong, take responsibility, be open, and find a way to remedy the situation or to prevent it from happening again. Hold yourself accountable.

Trust. Building trust requires a series of experiences that create a relationship over time. When we have challenges, they reveal people's efforts. It's about showing up. Our word is the only thing we have.

I don't want people working hard just to impress me; it's a turnoff. There is a way of showing who you are without pretense or arrogance. I want to see the real person. Some people are great test-takers but are not congruent in their actions. I want someone who is a hybrid of book smarts and street smarts.

Work ethic. Show an interest; put in the effort. Do your homework before a meeting. People on my team feel like part of a movement; they see where I'm going and want to go with me on that growth journey. The growth journey is a group purpose that we, as a team, are striving to accomplish. It can be as small as achieving our yearly sales goal or more long term, like becoming the number one real estate team in the city.

Surround yourself with positive people

Before we talk about skills and personalities, the most important thing is attitude and fit. Someone could have the perfect résumé and technical skills, but if their attitude is not in order, they can be the rotten apple that spoils the barrel. If you are short-staffed, it is easy to fall into the trap of hiring someone too quickly, when it would serve you better to listen to your gut and wait for the right person. In my case, I have made several mistakes in hiring someone for a support staff position who had greater ambitions. It was better to set them free to pursue their career ambitions rather than have them create resentment or negativity that would affect my team. I am particularly proud of one choice I made with an interviewee. This person was not a fit for my team, but when I referred him to a colleague, he became a main leader for my colleague's business and key to that company's success.

> **Wisdom quote from Jonathan Leary,
> CEO and founder of Remedy Place**
>
> "To stay creative and to keep dreaming big and staying positive: the
> dreaming big and the hype is really about being around an amazing
> team… Time is so valuable that I don't want to be around people who
> don't make me happy or inspire me or make me better. That's why
> that exchange of energy is so important."
>
> **YOUR INSIGHT** Who (among coaches, friends, consultants, col-
> leagues, staff) makes you and your organization better?

DISC assessment—personalities

Many entrepreneurs are motivated to achieve goals, and that's why
you're reading this book. It is likely that part of your personality
includes being something of a "driver." I am a driver, and my sister
has always called me "bossy," because that's part of who I am.

When I started in my real estate business, I partnered up with
someone who was also a driver with ego. We were both young, in our
20s, and had different ideas on what to do with our business. We com-
peted with each other, and it was not a strong, cohesive team. We split
up after a few years. Now, I choose people for my team who work with
me and not against me. Is it possible to have two drivers on one team?
As my mentor Rick Dergan says, "You can have two drivers on a team.
At least one of you needs to let go of your ego."

It is hard to drive a car or a team with more than one main driver.
A friend of mine is part of a big family in which everyone has strong
opinions, yet when the sisters sit in the car together, there can be
only one driver at the wheel. And they have learned that the sisters
who are passengers need to be quiet and not be "backseat drivers." It
wasn't easy when they were younger; they would argue about how the

driver should be driving. As they matured, they understood the practicality of getting along in a car. When these sisters cook a big family meal together, it is an excellent and memorable feast their friends can appreciate, because the sisters collaborate on who is providing which dishes and they fill in the gaps to make a complete meal, matching the quality of a nine-course menu at a top restaurant.

When you are a leader, you need clarity and good communication about who is in charge of what responsibilities. Even if everyone could be a good driver, each member needs to know their strengths and their role within the team.

So I have been speaking a lot about drivers, but there are other types and combinations of personalities in this popular assessment called DISC. Rick has built many teams and offices using this assessment, and when he first hired me, I took the DISC assessment. I have used it for building my own teams ever since. By now, you probably know what the D in DISC stands for: Driver. That's my main personality type, complemented by a healthy dose of I for Influencer. Influencers are optimistic, outgoing, and share openly. It makes me happy to introduce colleagues to each other. I am willing to share my successes and challenges so people can learn from my mistakes.

I have someone on my team who has more capacity for clients who want a long, leisurely lunch meeting, and she enjoys these meetings. Since I tend to eat quickly and long lunch meetings are not my strength, in order to improve my client relationships, I need this type of person—known as an Influencer—on my team. She is a good host, a talker, and very likable. She is the one who will throw a party and wants to make sure everyone is having a good time. She's a good friend to have. One weakness of this personality type is that they might spend too much of their time being social, or need to learn to be more consistent in their work.

Next in the quadrant is the Steady personality. This person goes with the flow and is a great team member, a good sidekick to the driver. They are agreeable to the group dynamics and help pitch in for whatever the group needs. They are the rock and help stabilize a team with their consistency and loyalty. The Steady personality has sensitivity and good listening skills. However, this person is less likely to take risks, might struggle with making decisions or resist change, and has difficulty establishing priorities. You will need this person on your team, but they are less likely to be the team leader.

The final category is the Compliant personality. This person is detail-oriented, cautious, and careful, and is good for your quality control. They help you establish and execute systems. They might not be as ambitious as Drivers, but you need them on your team. This person is likely to be more conscientious and attentive than your other types. Be sure to create opportunities to check in with this person so you have an open channel of communication with them, as they like to avoid conflict and might not share their feelings.

I've presented only a quick overview of the DISC personality assessment here, and I encourage you to dive deeper. There are links provided in the References section to multiple websites where you can get free or paid assessments.

Below are some of my thoughts on DISC personalities as reflected in popular culture. Feel free to discuss this with your team and add other characters to the list and send in your ideas to our social media so we can share your ideas with other readers!

D · DRIVER/DOMINANT	**I · INFLUENCER**
Tends to be the hero of a movie or story Greatest fear: being taken advantage of	Tends to be the party host Greatest fear: rejection

S · STEADY	**C · COMPLIANT**
Tends to be a good sidekick to the Driver Greatest fear: loss of security	Tends to be a quality control team member Greatest fear: criticism and being wrong

The Simpsons

Marge Simpson—SC: Values stability and cultural norms. She pays a lot of attention to detail. Does not seek position or authority. Has lots of internal emotions.

Bart Simpson—DI: Risk taker and great people person. Everyone loves Bart! Not agreeable to rules and regulations. Desires quick results and is a straight shooter.

Homer Simpson—I: Loves new adventures and is always excited. Has a big social aspect to him and thrives around a lot of people. Loves a good party.

Lisa Simpson—SC: Caring, sensitive, gentle, and loves helping others. She is empathetic and a great listener.

Bridgerton

Anthony Bridgerton—D: A natural leader of the Bridgerton family. He fears loss of control of his sister Daphne's courting and likes to take matters into his own hands.

Penelope Featherington—I: Very charming and fears social rejection or being ignored. Shows her enthusiasm about people in her community.

Daphne Bridgerton—S: Loves being supportive of her family and is motivated to help people. She is a team player and tries not to offend anyone.

Simon Basset—C: Skeptical of the world and analyzes everyone and everything, especially his feelings towards Daphne. Stability is very important to him.

The Office

Michael Scott—DI: The entertainer who loves being the center of attention with his jokes that make no sense. Likes breaking the rules and following the beat of his own drum. Is quite the socializer.

Dwight Schrute—DS: His strong will and confidence drive him to lead. He thrives amid routine and in uncluttered environments and has a strong distaste for unorganized and lazy coworkers.

Jim Halpert—S: Finds satisfaction in learning new ways to move up in his career. He values debate and can't resist an intellectual challenge; he argues for sport.

Pam Beesly—S: Dedicated and a warm protector, always ready to defend her loved ones. This is most apparent in her relationship with Jim. Although generally unenthusiastic about her job, her cheerful demeanor makes up for it. Finds comfort in routine.

Andy Bernard—I: Super social and loves positive attention from his family, friends, and coworkers. Doesn't like to be ignored and shows appreciation in thoughtful ways.

Star Wars

Darth Vader—DS: Diplomatic, strategic, systematic, a natural born leader. Focuses on results and goes about getting them in the most efficient way.

Princess Leia—DS: Also a natural born leader, intelligent and well informed. Has a great deal of confidence and reaches her goals with excellence.

Luke Skywalker—SI: Introspective, creative, and highly idealistic. Shows interest in helping others and is very adaptive. Very laid-back.

Yoda—SC: Logical, original, and very reserved. Strong ability to stick to a task and is known for building sophisticated plans and improving the lives of others.

Chewbacca—ID: Independent and adventurous. Very spontaneous and loves to live in the moment. Loyal to his friends and loves a good time. Also known for getting stuff done.

Harry Potter

Harry Potter—DC: The independent soul who loves adventure. He does not follow rules, as he feels that they prohibit you from being you. Very logical in organizing his thoughts and facts and values efficiency. Doesn't really care about attention and praise.

Albus Dumbledore—DI: An inspirational leader who loves helping his students reach their potential. Very empathetic, warm, and responsive in groups. Highly attuned to the emotions, needs, and motivations of others.

Ron Weasley—IS: Enthusiastic, energetic, and full of life! Very adaptable to many situations and always looks for the silver lining. Loves working in teams and being with friends.

Hermione Granger—SC: A deeply passionate soul who is systematic in solving problems and correcting others. A natural born thinker who often gets lost in her thoughts. Very calm and always seeking information.

Take a look at your team. If you need to have better systems in place, perhaps you should get more team members of the Compliant personality type. If you are a team leader and think more like an Influencer, perhaps you need to find a consultant with a Driver personality to help you design a strategic plan or a leadership coach to help you inspire your team with vision. Whatever your personality type, there are ways you can turn on the other parts of your brain to help you see the different needs of your business and also bring in help to fill in your gaps.

Team HOTS—character archetypes

As a leader, I prefer to focus on developing creative ideas, producing new projects, and inspiring my team. Even though I have a CPA designation and an accounting career in my past, that is the kind of detail-oriented and repetitive work I don't want to do anymore. It is better to hand off those kinds of tasks to someone who enjoys and excels at managing details.

Just because you have the skills or experience doesn't mean that is your character strength. You have to care and want to be doing it to give it your best. As my mentor Fran Hughes says in her advice: "You need to live your life in a want-to, choose-to-like-it, love-it basis. If you do anything because you want to choose to do it, you're there 100 percent."

HOTS is an acronym for a team from the book *One Minute Millionaire* by Mark Victor Hansen and Robert Allen, who are creators of the Chicken Soup for the Soul series. Each of the letters stands for an animal archetype you need for a successful team (Hare, Owl, Tortoise, and Squirrel). No matter what culture you come from, we think of animals as having certain characteristics from the folklore we have heard, and this is where this type of assessment is universal. The story of the tortoise and the hare is a well-known lesson, and it is about balance when you're forming a team. If you go too fast, you'll miss the details. If you go too slow, the project might not get completed. There is something important to learn from each kind of animal.

In this HOTS assessment, I prefer to do creative work like a Hare and hand off Squirrel-type work to others. Even though I don't prefer Squirrel work, it is important and still needs to be done, so I need to find someone competent on my team to get that kind of work completed. Without the full spectrum of the four types of animals from HOTS, my team would be short of some skills and perspectives needed for success.

I have a cinematographer friend, Danna Kinsky, who identifies as a Tortoise. She is fantastic when it comes to filming footage and sees technical details that should be captured. In a recent shoot, the director had to leave the set for a family emergency and Danna was able to step in to manage the set and continue the production, using the Hare and Owl parts of her brain. She couldn't do it all and still needed to direct a good number of people to carry out other tasks. In Danna's ideal world, she needs a writer to develop the story, a director to guide the shoot, and a producing team to organize the logistics and financing. Her preference is to show up with her equipment and be the camera operator or director of photography. While she is *able* to manage the whole set, that is not her preference; she chooses to stay behind the camera, where she excels and experiences her highest passion.

Let's say, for example, you want to form a company that makes some kind of product, whether it be women's purses or coffee mugs. As team leader, you don't necessarily need to be a certain type of personality of Team HOTS. You can fall anywhere in the four types. Most people will have a dominant animal type with a secondary aspect. You'll need someone to help you be the creative designer (Hare), someone to manage operations (Owl), someone to manage quality control (Tortoise), and someone to count the widgets and do accounting (Squirrel).

Here are typical roles the HOTS team might play in a purse company.

H · HARE	**O · OWL**
Jumping with ideas. Not all ideas should be executed. Needs a team to help them follow through on a project.	Flies high and sees a good overview of the forest. Good at seeing the big picture and future forecasting. Excels at strategy.
Roles: CEO, Marketing, Creative, Product Design	Roles: Operations, Customer Relations, Distribution, Strategy
T · TORTOISE	**S · SQUIRREL**
Sees close to the ground. Strong critical thinking and can identify possible flaws. Could be mistaken as negative. Detail-oriented, present-focused.	Happy with repetitive tasks such as counting widgets, bookkeeping, or fixing equipment. Good for sewing, making lots of phone calls, or organizing the mailing list.
Roles: Quality Control, Proofreader, Executive Assistant, Scheduling	Roles: Finance, Inventory, Manufacturing

- Where do you fall in the HOTS archetypes? What's your dominant animal and what is your secondary?

- What types of people do you prefer to hang out with? Can you identify where they fall in HOTS?

- What HOTS types do you currently have on your team?

- What HOTS types do you need to recruit to help strengthen your team?

Other team assessment tools

The assessment tools covered in this chapter were chosen because they are relatively easy to understand. In the case of the DISC, I have used it as my primary assessment tool for building my team. Other assessment tools require more study than we have time for in this book. They are good for self-awareness and also for improving communication and teamwork.

The Myers–Briggs test, with 16 different personality types, is helpful for learning different work and communication styles within a team. For example, if you find that certain members do not contribute to the discussion in big meetings, this is a good assessment to use to figure out how to best bring their contributions to your project efforts. The Enneagram has 9 personality types, with one dominant aspect and a secondary wing. My Enneagram shows I'm a 3, the Achiever, with a wing of 4, the Individualist. Depending on someone's development, they might change personality types over time. Knowing the personality types or work styles of your team members will help you lead a more cohesive organization.

Appreciative Inquiry is a managerial method where you focus on building on people's strengths, inspiration, and the strong connections between people rather than looking at deficiencies. Often, we get drawn to negative analysis or problem-solving modes. If you want to inspire positivity, it helps to build on the strengths and things that excite the group. What you focus on is what you build on. We have quickly mentioned some methods in this chapter. Please look at the References, which has links to resources so you can dive deeper into what interests you, and choose which assessment tools work best for you and your team.

My mentor Fran Hughes has focused on choosing members without these assessment tools, preferring to go with her gut feeling and excitement about someone's personality. My mentor Rick Dergan has successfully built many teams using only the DISC assessment and a few key questions highlighted in his interview. These resources are here for your learning, and you can decide how best to choose your team to manage and grow your organization.

Advice from my early mentors

Fran Hughes is a spiritual, dynamic leader who discovered she could change her beliefs about herself through affirmations and visualization. And since she could change herself, she wanted to help people grow to their higher potential. She met me after she lost her son in military duty and she had made it a personal priority to find young people to mentor. She was my mentor in the beginning of my real estate career, and to this day she is very generous in sharing her advice. Fran has a true passion for mentoring people even though we don't work in the same office. She likes to say she's in the business of "growing people." Fran is an excellent inspirational mentor.

Wisdom quotes from Fran Hughes, vice president and branch manager, real estate

Since 1978, Fran Hughes, a Society of Excellence Manager and Mayor's Award winner, has specialized and excelled in the marketing and sale of single-family homes and multi-residential properties on the Westside of Los Angeles.

On team leadership and mentoring

"You act in accordance to your beliefs... That's the problem—your beliefs were put in by other people. [It's] the stories you tell yourself. Once you learn how your mind works, and how your subconscious operates, you can change your own picture... I realized I could change my life and then I could change other people's lives. If I got you to believe in how I saw you, in the belief systems I knew you were capable of, that is the road to change."

YOUR INSIGHT What belief systems serve you and what limiting belief systems do you need to clean out?

Shadow and train

"The best people to train the young people are the top producers. To this day, I still have the top producers as mentors. New people start to shadow on day one, so they go on work appointments and imprint right away. The more you teach, the more you train, the better you get."

YOUR INSIGHT Who on your team can mentor and shadow each other? Do you have people you would like to shadow?

On self-improvement and attitude

"I don't go to sleep or get out of bed in the morning before I run my affirmations. I live in abundance... I always find joy... I love the game. I love the negotiation. I'm still having fun."

YOUR INSIGHT Do you run affirmations? How do you find joy as you affirm your day?

What makes someone coachable?

"There's such a difference between people who are interested and people who are committed... When somebody excites me, then I know they can excite other people... I like people who are really bright. I don't do drama. No prima donnas. You want drama, go to the theater!"

YOUR INSIGHT How are you coachable? Are people on your team coachable?

When I switched real estate companies, Rick Dergan was my new manager and generously took me under his wing. He is more of a scientist, who says "the proof is in the pudding." As with my mentor Fran, we have a strong connection that has outlasted our office relationship. We have become lifelong friends who give back to each other. I share my strengths with tech and social media with him, and he continues to share his wisdom and advice with me, especially when I need to hire the right fit for my team. Rick is a very systems- and process-oriented coach who changed my mindset to see my work as an entrepreneur and grow my business.

Wisdom quotes from Rick Dergan, operating partner, real estate

Rick Dergan has been in the real estate business for over 35 years, running multiple offices in the Los Angeles area. He is a top producer among realtors and currently dominates the beachside market.

Why teams are powerful

"I have teams that have 10 to 15 people on them. The marketing budget for a team is much bigger [and more competitive]. In the future, my teams will be 15 to 20 people."

YOUR INSIGHT How can your team be powerful and outdo the competition?

Use assessment tools and find people with goals

"DISC test is 25 percent of the hiring process—shows strengths and weaknesses. I've hired people who did well on the test but not great on the job. I ask them: It's 2024, and you've had the best three years of your life. Tell me, what has happened? Only 10 percent of the people get that question. The ones who get it are really good. They have goals, know where they want to be. I want the one who is fully charged. What kind of car are you driving, where are you living?"

YOUR INSIGHT Do people in your organization have goals? Are they "charged" with internal motivation?

Advice on running a strong organization

"How do you know people are sharing your vision? You gotta really share your vision weekly. Share what you want to accomplish this week. Ask them what they want to accomplish this week. As team leader, you have the bigger vision, [the] ultimate goal. Use the 4-1-1: 4 weeks, 1 quarter, 1 year. Keep them focused on the 1-year plan, and how close are we to accomplishing that 1-year plan?"

YOUR INSIGHT Do you have a clear vision that you are communicating for each time period: 4 weeks, 1 quarter, 1 year?

Advice for a new entrepreneur

"Don't run by ego. Ego will ruin your business. I'm having so much fun building my team... Failure is okay. It's how you get up. Every time I fail, I get up stronger. If you don't fail, you're not growing. It's not how you fell down, it's how you get up."

YOUR INSIGHT How can you look at your failures as opportunities to get stronger and to grow? Are you willing to fall down? Are there risks you are resisting that maybe you should take?

EXERCISES

If you don't know your personality traits, take the assessments for DISC, Myers–Briggs, and other personality tests that appeal to you.

- Assess who in your life supports you personally and/or professionally. Name the top five people who are in your inner circle. Are they reliably your "ride or die" types? If not, look harder and identify others with whom you can build deeper relationships to bring them more into your inner circle.

- What personality traits do you want your inner circle to have so they can support you? Does your inner circle have them? For example, if you're a strong D, do you have people in the other parts of the DISC who round you out? If you're a strong H, do you have people who represent the other personalities in HOTS?

- Name people in the middle and outer circles of your network. What do they offer to help you with your brand or your goals? Who do you want to bring into your "team" to strengthen your brand?

- Are there people in your circle you may have outgrown? What are their negative qualities that you want to disassociate from? Is there anyone else who has those negative qualities, and how can you amplify the better qualities by building new relationships or becoming closer with another type of person?

- Do you want a mentor with certain skills or qualities? Write down your vision of what a mentor can be like. Do they have the personality of an enthusiastic cheerleader, or are they going to give you tough love? Do you want someone to help you manage your time better, or give you a different kind of skill, for example, negotiating? Is this person already in your network, perhaps a friend who has professional skills in marketing who could help you learn more about marketing?

- If it is not obvious who this mentor could be, name five ways you can find this mentor. For example: make a list of successful people with whom you have common interests and ask each of them for an informational interview.

8

PACKAGING PRODUCT: WHAT ARE YOUR COLORS?

La presentación siempre es importante.
(Presentation is always important.)

MY MOM

You are what you wear

GOT THIS obsession with presentation and packaging from my mom, who made sure everything from our dinner plates to our wardrobe styling was well put together. My mom said that when I wore a red shirt, I looked more handsome to her. She thought my sister looked most beautiful in white. Our food was always made colorful with garnish. Other people might have a bowl of beans, but my mom would top it off with avocado slices, Mexican cheese, and sour cream to make it look as though it came from a five-star restaurant.

Early on, as a young boy, I was obsessed with making sure my hair looked good. And I feel more confident when I put myself in a suit, especially when I wear navy. The minute I walk out of my home, I don't know who I'm going to run into, so I need to make sure I feel good in my packaging and proud of my attire. What I wear and how I feel in my personal packaging is part of my brand. When I meet new clients or go to an event, I make sure I feel confident in how I present myself. The accessories I wear, such as my watch, shoes, and belt, represent my attention to detail. My packaging tells the world that I care about what I look like, and this shows I am an elevated brand.

Not only is my personal packaging important but also my product packaging. All of my marketing materials have a consistent color, consistent theme, consistent quality of material. I love all of my marketing materials to be soft to the touch. All the details matter. Make sure your presentation and packaging have intention behind them. First impressions matter in any industry. Make sure that your packaging is at 100 percent.

Case study: Leon Wu, CEO and founder of Sharpe Suiting

In 2013, Sharpe Suiting trademarked a term, "andropometrics," which refers to custom-designed bespoke clothes for gender-neutral and genderqueer fashion to fit people of all sizes and genders. The company's mission is to help people showcase who they are and elevate their lives with their fashion. Besides being featured in NY and LA fashion shows and at entertainment events such as the Oscars and Emmys, they have a charitable service component of the company to support the LGBTQ community, women, and people of color. As they dress cultural trailblazers and get recognition for tailored suits and formal wear, they also describe their environmental commitment and labor practices on their website to reflect their values.

"As a queer designer I'm able to see fashion outside of the box. Identity is based on experiences, and because I've experienced the shame, frustration, and anxiety—genderqueer-bodied people often do— I wanted to create not just a clothing line to fill the lack but a place to rectify this issue of not being welcomed or accepted... One of the Sharpe signature touches is the contrast double buttonhole on the lapel to symbolize the equality sign."

YOUR INSIGHT

- How would you like to elevate your look to better express your brand or identity? Would you like to find ways to customize your fashion, either with accessories or with custom tailoring? If you find it difficult to find clothes for your body shape, are there boutique designers or a favorite tailor who can fit you better? What do you need to do to feel more proud and confident in your personal package?

- Reflect on how Sharpe Suiting creatively serves a niche market. Are you part of an audience that isn't being served in your business? How do you better serve this underserved audience?

Embrace stories that mean something to you

When I was choosing iconic LA locations for my photo shoot with my big office desk, I chose landmarks that meant something to me personally. Los Angeles County Museum of Art and the Walt Disney Concert Hall were at the top of my list because I remember how hard I worked as a caterer at events hosted at those venues when I was first launching my real estate career. My workday was fully booked with two jobs back-to-back: I worked at the real estate office during the day and did my catering job at night. As I was designing printed brochures that featured photos from that shoot, I did not want to use a generic LA palm trees photo on the cover. I chose the streetlights sculpture at LACMA because it was there that I made the hard choice to quit my catering job, with nothing to fall back on for income. I saw my real estate mentor at that event and I did not want her to see me, knowing that being dressed and working as a caterer would confuse my branding and commitment to my real estate career. Remembering my struggles keeps me humble and aligned to my strong work ethic, but that photo is uniquely meaningful to me. Anyone could put palm trees on the cover of their brochure, but that photo from LACMA has a story behind it. It represents the start of my full commitment to my new career, with nothing to fall back on.

Similarly, Janelle Monáe humbly remembers how she grew up and wants to pay tribute to the working-class people in her family who wore uniforms. How she styles her wardrobe in her music videos and performances is a constant reminder to her audience of who she wants to honor.

Wisdom quote from Janelle Monáe, singer, songwriter, and actor

"When I started my musical career, I was a maid, I used to clean houses. My parents—my mother was a proud janitor, my stepfather who raised me like his very own worked at the post office and my father was a trash man. They all wore uniforms. And that's why I stand here today in my black and white and I wear my uniform to honor them."

YOUR INSIGHT Is there something meaningful from your life that can inspire a unique style? Whether that's your fashion or product packaging, is there something from your identity that can translate into a brand?

Customize the experience for your clients

Early in my real estate career, I worked with a client who had relocated from New York. Sarah was looking in a specific area of Los Angeles that reminded her of the house where she grew up in New York. Based on her descriptions, I followed my gut instinct and matched her to a modest middle-class home that I thought would be perfect for her. As soon as Sarah walked into the home, her eyes lit up. She put her hands on her cheeks in amazement and said, "Wow, Ivan, this looks exactly like the dining room where I grew up. I can almost smell the pizza and pasta that we would have every Friday night." Both of her parents had already passed, so I could tell there was an emotional attachment to this special childhood memory that she now associated with her new home in Los Angeles.

I wanted to do something special for her, so I asked Sarah what her favorite pizza and pasta and toppings were. After we closed escrow, as soon as I got the keys, I went to a local New York pizzeria to get her favorite pizza with mushrooms and pepperoni and her favorite pasta with pesto. I set up her favorite food in the dining room of her new home to re-create the fond memories of her childhood. As I was waiting for her in the dining room, I heard the front door open and immediately heard her crying as she smelled the New York memories from the front door.

As she walked into the dining room with tears rolling down her cheeks, she exclaimed with disbelief, "No, Ivan. No, you didn't." Yes, yes, I did. I was celebrating her in a unique and personal way. That day was more than handing her keys to her new home; to me it was all about packaging that experience in a way she would never forget. Packaging doesn't have to be just your external packaging or your product packaging. I share this story to illustrate how you can package an unforgettable experience that sets your brand apart from anything else.

Food carries great memories for people, and it is no wonder that we associate relationships and special occasions with our favorite chocolate, cupcakes, or something special. And if you can identify what delights your clients and collaborators, you can find the perfect thank-you or birthday gift to help you build your brand. Sugarfina candies and Sprinkles cupcakes are top favorites in Beverly Hills, with their excellent packaging. Sprinkles can customize their cupcakes to spell out someone's name or feature colors that celebrate a favorite sports team. Another company that does an excellent job of packaging is a chocolatier that takes branding seriously. They will custom-print the branding of your company on their delicious chocolates. Compartés Chocolatier is an impressive chocolate brand that also sets itself apart. Whether or not you're a chocolate fan, you are bound to remember their artfully decorated bars and custom-printed logos. Their packaging and design make them meaningful and unforgettable.

Case Study: Compartés Chocolatier

Not only is Compartés a premium gourmet chocolate, handmade from scratch in artistic designs, but it is also a firm that offers custom printing on its chocolates to create edible art and gifts. Clients such as Gucci, Netflix, and American Express have commissioned their logos to be printed on Compartés chocolates for their events and gifts. A company that has been around since 1950, its famous fans have included Marilyn Monroe, Frank Sinatra, Elvis Presley, the Kennedys, and Winston Churchill.

YOUR INSIGHT How can you customize your product or packaging to better serve your clients? What can you do to further differentiate your brand?

Choose your roles and the company you keep

The entertainment world exemplifies on a grand scale the more difficult aspects of branding and entrepreneurship that a more traditional business might also have to face. When an actor chooses to be on a particular show, that role becomes a big part of their image. Will they get typecast as that kind of character in other projects? Or can they portray other aspects of their abilities so they can have a variety of roles and a bigger career? As they work through their branding challenges, the public eye is on their every move. Sometimes actors get involved in a controversy in their personal life or get associated with an image based on the company they keep. With so much attention on their choices, they need to be strategic about what events they attend and have help with their branding.

This brings to mind my friend Doyle Rice, who is a talent manager. He started out as an actor and loved giving his actor friends advice.

Eventually, he realized that his true passion was talent management. He knows from personal experience what his clients face, and that is part of his success as a talent manager. I'm sharing with you some gems from my interview with Doyle.

Wisdom quotes from Doyle Rice, talent manager

Doyle began his career as a talent manager when he started a youth talent division at his friend's agency. Now he owns his own company, Royle Dice, representing actors including Isabella Gómez (*Modern Family, One Day at a Time*) and Odessa A'zion (*Fam, Grand Army*).

Be strategic in developing your fans

"[For actors], you want to have your fans and I want casting directors to be your fans. Casting directors will love you, they become your big fans, and they're going to bring you into the room. Even if you don't book that project, it's okay. They're going to bring you back into producers and eventually [you'll get] your role."

YOUR INSIGHT Who are your strategic allies? Maybe they don't have clients or projects for you right now, but they have successful careers. How can you develop a relationship with them to help your career grow?

Build your brand to be multifaceted and contribute towards representation

"I think that building a great brand has diversity and [involves] making sure that you don't get stuck under one umbrella or one type of character... A great way to build a brand that shows representation matters. I don't think that people should always be playing maids or drug dealers or anything like that. Or playing just someone from the hood and never [playing] a doctor role.

"Representation really matters, and people who stick to their guns… Isabella Gómez is definitely one of them. She does not play any kind of maid roles. She does not play any kind of drug cartel roles, because she's from Colombia, and she doesn't want that representation."

YOUR INSIGHT What values do you stand for, and what do you need to stand against?

Showcase your greatness

Personally, I update my headshots often, especially as I expand my brand. Some entertainers take different headshots with different photographers to find ways to capture their different personas. Some actors will take a new headshot with the right beard or haircut for the role they are auditioning for, so they look the part. By dressing and grooming for the role, they are making it easy for someone to see their potential and how great they would be in that part.

Taking a page from how actors find a way to stand out from the big pool of applicants in Los Angeles, I want you to figure out how to showcase your greatness. If you are new in your career, find photos of people in your field who are more advanced in their game. Remember to showcase your personality while you dress the part.

A friend of mine, Nicolette, is a photographer and life coach. Because of this combination of skills, she asks key questions *before* the photo shoot, in the planning meetings, about the client's desired branding image. This helps her be on the same page as the client about what they want the photo shoot to achieve. Not only does she have a different approach to doing headshots, she puts energy into her newsletters and social media in a way that shows she "walks the talk" of branding.

Wisdom quotes from Nicolette Jackson-Pownall, personal brand headshots photographer

Nicolette grew up in France and started as a photographer at a young age. After a career in sales, she pursued her lifelong passion in photography, developing her business and specializing in branding. Her unique experience in sales and as a life coach provides a point of view that helps her clients tune into their needs for their portrait and lifestyle sessions.

Be in dialogue with yourself and your photographer about branding

"Branding has been truly a problem-solving approach to portrait photography… Let's start with the authentic. Let's unbury and unpeel how you've been projecting yourself or how you think you need to project yourself… Really, what do you stand for? I try to understand their backstory. Why are you talking to me? Why are you in the process of looking for a photographer?… This is a dialogue."

YOUR INSIGHT If your photographer doesn't have branding in mind, can you answer these questions independently and then communicate your thoughts to your photographer so you can get better portraits?

Love your photos and see your greatness

"You deserve to have photos of yourself that you love. And to see reflected the greatness that has been there all along. Because once you see yourself in that light, there's no going back. You'll have the confidence to step into your version of success."

YOUR INSIGHT How can your headshots showcase your greatness? Are there backdrops or props you want to help step you into your success?

EXERCISES

• What colors make you feel like you? Do you have certain colors that make you feel more confident? Some power outfits that give you confidence? If you need help answering these questions, ask a friend who is known for having a good eye and is a supportive personality.

• Watch an episode of Tan France's *Dressing Funny* on YouTube. Comedians are so honest about their insecurities and their style challenges. This is where you can learn to be honest about your own insecurities. What are your insecurities? Are you afraid of looking like _____ (fill in the blank)?

• What type of personality or professional branding upgrade do you want? They say, if you want to be a CEO, then start dressing like a CEO. What type of person do you want to be respected as? At what events do you want to better present yourself?

• Tan France said that when he was young, he was inspired to start figuring out his personal style by looking to the style of David

Beckham. Who do you admire? Who has the style you want? This might be a combination of people. Create a "look book" by flipping through magazines and cutting out photos or colors, or create a digital vision board.

- Can you find a friend (or several) with that "tough love" to help you put together your new look? Someone you trust to push you out of your normal comfort zone and into what you want to look like? If you don't have someone who immediately comes to mind, ask for referrals.

- Create a mood board with your signature colors that you could use for your product packaging or as inspiration for your personal outfit styles.

- Keep a storage box with packaging you like from different companies you respect. This will serve as a file cabinet of ideas you might use later.

9

FINDING YOUR CREATIVITY: BE INSPIRED

If life knocks you down, try to
land on your back. Because
if you can look up, you can get up.

LES BROWN

Build something for fun

WAS A YOUNG builder. I loved building things as soon as I figured out what glue and tape could do for me. When I look back at these memories, they forecast how I would enjoy building a career and different parts of my business.

I was always looking inside books and trying to replicate the scenery of the illustrations using materials I could find around the house. I got into everything, anything I could get my hands on, which sometimes included my mom's earrings, pieces of her belts, or anything I could find in her magic drawers. In school, I was always the first to volunteer to build a diorama.

Dioramas and other school projects that required building meant my dad and I could spend time together bringing an art piece to life. One memorable project was building a castle. My dad took me to get cardboard from one of the grocery stores down the street. Because I was always looking for the perfect cardboard pieces, we had to go to several grocery stores. I was so picky—I wanted the right texture, the right length, and the right shape. My dad had a limited budget for these art projects, so he gave me $15 to buy whatever I needed, which included tape, paint, and glue to make these projects come to life. Everything else I used was free and found materials. I had to learn to be resourceful. My attention to detail was so specific that I carefully blended the paints to make the perfect shade of gray.

These days, I like to design my own furniture for my home and have it custom-built. I didn't go to art or design school, but I sketch out my designs and then find someone to build them for me. I get to pick out the fabrics or make my couch fit my space better than any store-bought couch. Each piece is special to my home, and no one else has it. There is a sense of pride when I see a finished product come from an idea I had in the beginning. Build something for fun! It could be a collage to contribute to your vision board or a centerpiece for your dinner table. It doesn't have to be a big project, but it can be as big as you want it to be.

Over 10 years ago, a friend took me to a barbecue hosted by Mark Batson. When I walked into his home, I saw a gorgeous grand piano and I knew I was in the home of an artist. I had no idea he was music royalty, but I knew we were going to be friends because he was such a humble person and we shared our strong passion for music in that first interaction. You can find out more about Mark in chapter 2.

Wisdom quotes from Mark Batson, music producer

How to be a successful creative person

"The key to being a successful creative person is to create. It takes a certain confidence level to sit down and put pen to paper, and face your fears... There are those voices that say maybe you shouldn't be doing this and stick to what you were doing. The main part of being creative is to defeat those voices. The most important thing: keep creating, keep developing your art, and keep learning about marketing."

YOUR INSIGHT What can you create every day? Some people like to try a new recipe or change up a recipe for something they already know how to bake. Some people like to keep a journal to write or sketch in. Make a commitment to be creative every day. What is that activity?

How to market successfully

"Marketing is knowing who your audience is and knowing how to reach them. Learn about who likes it, and make sure you keep delivering what your audience wants and needs."

YOUR INSIGHT Who do you think your audience is? Do you know how to reach them?

Constraints can be helpful

Just call me the child can collector. My mom used to take us on a walk every evening at 6 p.m. During these walks around the neighborhood I noticed a recycling center down the street. The recycling center had a sign: "Cans 5 cents. Bottles 3 cents. Newspapers 2 cents." That spurred a moneymaking idea in my young entrepreneurial mind.

I saw that my parents were throwing away cans and bottles in the trash and not getting money for them. So I started retrieving those recyclables and putting them in a different trash can as my personal stash to take to the recycling center. During our family evening walks, I also noticed that neighbors left cans and bottles in their recycling bins along the sidewalk every Tuesday for the trash pickup. I realized my neighbors were not cashing in on their cans and bottles, and that money could be mine!

Without my parents' consent, I woke at five in the morning, grabbed a bag from the garage, sneaked out the back door, and collected my neighbors' recyclables for about an hour. I knew my parents would be mad, so I hid my found treasures in one of our storage units out by the garage. Every week, I would take my bags to the recycling center and collect my earnings.

The owner of the recycling center asked me, "Wow, where are you getting all these cans, young boy? Your parents must drink a lot of soft drinks." My response was, "Yeah, we have a lot of parties; that's where I get all the cans." I didn't want to get in trouble and my parents didn't know I was waking up at five in the morning to be the child can collector. Because I was determined to earn money for my toys and my savings account, my creativity was exercised to deal with my constraints.

The moral of this story is that there are always opportunities around, you just have to be creative enough to identify them. Even as a kid I was able to connect the dots: Things that people threw away could be worth something. All I had to do was put in the sweat equity and collect the money that was otherwise being thrown away.

Wisdom quote from Austin Kleon, artist and author

Austin Kleon is the *New York Times*–bestselling author of a trilogy of illustrated books about creativity in the digital age: *Steal Like an Artist*, *Show Your Work!*, and *Keep Going*. He's also the author of *Newspaper Blackout*, a collection of poems made by redacting the newspaper with a permanent marker. His books have been translated into dozens of languages and have sold over a million copies worldwide.

Constraints can create genius

"In this age of information abundance and overload, those who get ahead will be the folks who figure out what to leave out, so they can concentrate on what's really important to them. Nothing is more paralyzing than the idea of limitless possibilities... The right constraints can lead to your very best work."

YOUR INSIGHT Think of a time when you built something with very little. What project can you give yourself today that might inspire something creative? This can be a short project, as quick as a five-minute drawing or building something out of scraps from around your home, starting with the toilet paper roll or items as small as toothpicks.

Egos kill inspiration

When you're driving for success, it is easy to feel disappointed that you did not get famous right away, or to take it personally if an important someone has not returned your phone call. If you fail at something, think of it as practice. Find your work ethic to try again. Look at how basketball players will practice shooting from the free throw lines and work on their success rate but don't expect success every time. When you have a success, don't let it go to your head or else you're indulging your ego. If you ignore your ego's desire to be seen, be careful that you don't act out on social media or at an event. Find ways to do something positive to get the acknowledgment your ego needs.

For example, I had a client whose house I was selling and my junior colleague was assisting me with that project. When he left my team, he took that client and sold that listing under his own business, and my ego jumped up and down, being angry and resentful. It was a downward spiral of damage that would go nowhere. I had to call a supportive friend to advise me how to get out of my own way. I did not want to spend more days being angry and waste precious time that I could invest in serving my other clients and being creative with my new marketing campaigns.

Wisdom quote from Questlove, musician, songwriter, and author

"Your ego is one of the things that need to be managed rather than indulged or ignored."

YOUR INSIGHT When was a recent time that your ego popped up? Were you able to manage it? If not, how could you have managed your ego better?

Set boundaries for creativity

Mark out time in your schedule to be creative. I put everything in my calendar. Time management is key to getting a lot accomplished. Put away your phone and other distractions; tell your family or others in your inner circle that you need to take time off or do a retreat. It can be just half a day, or you might pick a place to go for a few days for this creative time. It could be a staycation or just a day at the park. You can revisit chapter 4, "Invest in Yourself," to find ways to recharge and set up routines like journaling to have a daily practice or figure out how often you need to get away for your work–life balance.

I don't check emails or phone calls for two hours as part of my morning meditation and exercise routine. Those two hours are when I listen to podcasts or write in my journal to stimulate my creativity. Keeping my mind free of distractions allows me to do more with my time.

For my marketing efforts, I don't follow other real estate agents because I want to be more original in my content. Instead, I follow filmmakers, marketing and branding experts, and technology companies. By looking at other industry leaders who are out-of-the-box thinkers, I maintain my originality.

**Wisdom quote from Questlove,
musician, songwriter, and author**

"I believe in perpetuating a certain amount of mystery."

YOUR INSIGHT What do you want to keep mysterious or private about your public persona? What do you want to provide a teaser about to generate more mystery and intrigue around you and your work?

Manage your time

If you're an ambitious person like me, you want a lot of things out of life. However, it is hard to juggle more than three big projects that demand a lot of time. I was aware that when I made the commitment to write this book, create a video course, and produce my podcast, that would be three big projects to juggle on top of my main project of running my real estate business. I have learned so much doing these three projects, and sometimes I needed extra time to debrief and process more of what I learned from my new ventures.

This juggle meant I had to limit my social life and make a schedule that would handle the stresses of these demands. It meant I had to assess each social meeting and ask, "What am I really getting out of this? Can I fulfill my needs differently in a shorter amount of time so I'm not staying out too late and unable to recharge for my next demanding day?" Friends asked me to go away on a vacation, but could I really afford to be offline for five days, or was I going to be stressed trying to get a good Wi-Fi connection so I could work while at a resort? I said no. But I said yes to a friend's special occasion dinner, which meant a lot to me. The long dinner party moved my normally early bedtime to 1 a.m., so I had to plan to adjust my next day's schedule. These are the kinds of work–life balance questions I have to ask regularly in order to maintain the high level of productivity I expect of myself.

> ### Wisdom quote from Questlove, musician, songwriter, and author
>
> "Expect change. Demand change of yourself. Try, as always, to keep it within the bound of the attainable. There are many stresses in the creative life, so it's important to limit the self-inflicted ones."
>
> YOUR INSIGHT What kind of stress do you put on yourself? How can you reduce that self-inflicted stress?

Creativity as your fuel

Even though I went to accounting school, I kept doing things to nurture my creativity. Applying principles of what I learned to different parts of my life kept me whole. Skills I learned as a singer and performer allowed me to be creative and have a good rapport with people in my sales efforts. I collect different kinds of friends who reflect the different parts of me. I have a silly sense of humor that started when I was a kid playing pranks on my cousins and other family. This sense of joy is part of my brand. For instance, to break up my real estate posts, I might include a cute shot of my cockapoo dog, Noah. For Valentine's Day, I'll post a clip of myself singing a romantic ballad. For my real estate posts, I show my enthusiasm and engage my audience by tagging certain people to let them know I think that dream house would be perfect for them.

My whole family loves fun and music. I was thinking, who else in my family is creative and successful in their career? When the movie *Coco* arrived in theaters, everyone in my extended family went to see it—not only because we were proud it was a Mexican story but also because my cousin Paul worked on it. That film symbolized pride in our culture and our family. Not only is my cousin Paul an accomplished animator and team leader at Pixar, he also started a successful band as a teen in the San Francisco Bay Area. He still has a fan base for his music. He didn't have the easiest childhood, since he didn't grow up with his parents and had to help raise his younger brother. By the time he was 16, he was paying his own rent and working at Uncle Rigo's car dealership. His passions and creativity have given him the fuel to get through his difficult times and shine as a high achiever, bringing him success in his career.

Wisdom quotes from Paul Mendoza, lead animator and musician

Paul Mendoza started his creative career as a musician in the San Francisco Bay Area. There were limitations on what he could afford to pay for college and he took classes in animation at a local community college. A friend working in the mail room at Pixar said they needed help at work and he took a job there, doing whatever they needed. That was in 1997. Paul dropped out of college to become a full-time animator there; he was the first Mexican animator on their staff. He led the cultural research for the movie *Coco*, and some of the story lines are based on his personal story and our family connection to Michoacán, Mexico. Paul has been the lead animator at Pixar for Oscar-winning films such as *Coco*, *Toy Story 4*, *Cars*, and *Ratatouille*.

Creativity as sanity

"The only thing that kept me sane was music, that was the only structure I had. I loved writing it, I loved writing about it, I loved the
expression in it. When I got into animation, it felt like the same thing
to me from an expression standpoint, where I'm able to express what
a character is feeling emotionally."

YOUR INSIGHT Is there something creative that can help you feel
centered and be your go-to activity in times of stress?

Find a creative community to work with

"I loved the passion of the other animators at Pixar. We were all brand-
new, very scrappy, we all loved film, and I loved that. I wanted to be
a part of it. It was a hard decision and I got a lot of grief for it, from
animators especially. They'd say to me, 'You gave up the music industry for this crap?' and I'd say, 'Well, yeah! This crap is pretty cool.'"

YOUR INSIGHT If you're choosing between different creative
options, decide if the teams you will be working with fit you well.
Do you need community to support your creativity? Some writers
or artists will join a Zoom "virtual office hours" class to get group
support. Sometimes the facilitator will give the group a prompt as
a way to unexpectedly spark new work.

How to stay creative: Take a break and go to different environments

"My brain tends to talk a lot. And I think the biggest thing is thinking
about how to capture that—whether it be writing it down, sketching
it out, or calling my answering machine and leaving myself a message.
A lot of the time, after I go for a run, I'll lay down on the [yoga] mat for

10 minutes and I'll just stare at a wall. Sometimes in our busy lifestyles we really need time to just stare at a wall. And I think that's okay. The hard part is telling yourself that that's okay to do. I struggle to tell myself to spend 5 to 10 minutes a day just staring at a wall.

"Coffee is my religion. It's the ritual of it. It's not really the caffeine. I love the idea of going somewhere, sitting at a coffee shop, and sketching somebody at the other end of the table. That's one of the ways I meditate. I can just observe. That's what artists do; it's their greatest skill—not the singing, not the drawing or the playing guitar. It's observing."

YOUR INSIGHT Do you need to give yourself permission to take a break? What does that look like? Do you have a ritual or place that helps you be creative or meditate?

Expect the unpredictable

Part of being open-minded is welcoming unexpected and unpredictable outcomes. The creative process is far from a straight line. Sometimes you spend all this time on a project only to decide it is not the direction you want to go, and you need to start over from the beginning. It might be frustrating to have lost time, but we need to roll with it and not think of it as rejection. I am so excited to be able to share an interview with a senior design consultant in my social network, David Bamber. This Englishman is not only highly accomplished and creative, he has also worked closely with Tom Ford, the eponymous fashion designer who represents an age-defying classic style I am a big fan of.

Wisdom quotes from David Bamber, design consultant

David Bamber is Tom Ford's design studio director and also made a splash with his *Firebird* costume design for the English National Ballet. He is humble and not one to be in the spotlight, and thus does not often give interviews. Here are some quotes from a rare and treasured interview with him.

Show your personality

"When I look at a young person's portfolio, I try really hard to see the individual in there and not what they can produce on a computer… I want to see the portfolios talk to me. Fashion is all about appearances and attitude… You have to try and read the personality when you're looking at work."

YOUR INSIGHT Do you let your personality shine through in your work? If not, how can you infuse more of your personality into your projects?

You're as good as you think you are

"If you're really interested in doing something, find the way to do it, to approach it. I have gone through so many examples of when some-body else could have talked me out of it by telling me that I wasn't good enough. You are as good as you think you are. You have to keep going against that until you come up against a barrier… You have to believe in your own ability to drive yourself forward. It's not just your ability. It's your sense of being… Use your enthusiasm. Use your energy… There's always something that inspires you to keep going."

> **YOUR INSIGHT** Is your self-assessment accurate? Do you need help or a support system to encourage your creativity? How good do you want to be?

Do something unrelated

Many musicians also paint. Many dancers also like to design clothing or bags. While I am trained as a singer and have taken dance lessons, I have always liked figuring out what clothes to wear and I admire great fashion designers. I have used my personal interest in interior design to draw designs for my home, so I can have custom-built furniture. I feel the joy of accomplishing something new, or building something that no one else has. Find your joys, and if you don't know what they might be, dig into your childhood and think of what you used to do for fun as a kid. Maybe it was building dioramas like me, or maybe you sewed clothes for your stuffed animals. Creativity is using your child's mind.

Not only is learning a new skill good for your creativity, it also has anti-aging aspects as we get older. This is because it keeps you on your toes. A friend of mine had a grandfather who had Alzheimer's, so she has made a commitment to learn a new skill every year to improve neuroplasticity and train her memory. This commitment has led her to learn more than one skill every year! From freestyle rapping to producing puppet shows, there are a variety of skills one might not expect to learn. What's her secret? Curiosity. When she meets a new friend, she finds out what they do for fun and how they do it. One thing leads to another creative possibility.

Check in with yourself every few months to make sure you're not in a creative rut.

Wisdom quotes from Valentina Vee, filmmaker

Valentina Vee is a filmmaker based in Los Angeles. More of her bio is in chapter 6, "Social Media Influence."

Learn about cultures

"I try to go to a museum in every place that I visit, to learn about the culture, to learn about the place."

YOUR INSIGHT How do you learn about different cultures? If you don't travel internationally, what are other ways you can learn about different cultures? Friends, podcasts, and documentaries are my favorite ways to learn.

Mix it up

"Learn other forms of art, don't be afraid to be curious, don't be afraid to learn, don't be afraid to be a student of the world."

YOUR INSIGHT Is there another art form you're curious about? Is there something that feels difficult and out of reach? Find a friend who is good at that kind of art and have them give you a field trip or an orientation.

EXERCISES

- Attend events that have nothing to do with your business. I have been able to gain a competitive advantage over other colleagues by looking at what other brands in different industries were doing.

- Make a list of three to five new skills you might want to learn. Find out how you can learn those skills and make a commitment to start one this month.

- Create a board of all the things that inspire you. These could be objects like tiles from Morocco, or spices from India, or flowers from Hawaii. Or they could be local things like the tree from your childhood home, or an action figure toy or miniature space shuttle.

- Shake it up! Attend and observe in a different environment from your normal world, something outside your discipline. If you are a writer, go attend a music concert or listen to some new bands via virtual concerts; you might hear words that stimulate your vocabulary or concepts. If you are a designer, go to a dance event; the costumes and lighting might trigger a different way of seeing shapes. If you want to study product packaging, go to an ethnic grocery store and see how other cultures package items.

- Find your pick-me-up. Let's say you don't feel inspired or social. While it's best to shake up your environment, there are shows that take you around the world without you leaving the house. For example, look at shows on Netflix like *Amazing Hotels*, *The World's Most Extraordinary Homes*, or *Chef's Table*. Or do some research on natural phenomena like the aurora borealis (northern lights) or read about something you like, such as the top 10 largest waterfalls or some animals you like from the National Geographic site or the Sierra Club.

- Get active! Learn a new skill such as a new dance or learn to sing a new song. You don't need to perform it for anyone if you don't want to. The point is to use different parts of your brain. If you want to do something more interactive, take an improv or acting class where you learn to interact intimately with a roomful of "strangers" who are also there to learn.

- Plan some travels. Even if you don't have the budget or opportunity to travel soon, planning your next trip or two gets you to read about different cultures and geographies, and this might lead to you seeing a new design or hearing about a new way of doing things.

10

COLLABORATIONS AND RELATIONSHIPS

Competition starts me at the race.
Collaboration gets me to the finish line.

JEN CHENG

Competition and collaboration

MY HIGH SCHOOL friend's parents had a senior care assisted living facility in my neighborhood. I had the idea of partnering with my friend to set up a soda vending machine business at the center. We could provide better prices retailing soft drinks we bought in bulk instead of the seniors leaving the facility to buy a soda for twice as much at the corner store. However, I personally did not have the start-up capital to set up a vending machine. My friend's dad offered to buy and set up three vending machines if we teens would do the physical labor for the once-a-week maintenance of restocking and accounting. We would split the profits, and it would be a win-win for everyone, including our customers. My friend's dad did not have the time to manage the maintenance, and we did not have the start-up capital for the machines. Leveraging our resources of time and capital, we made a profitable team. If you see a customer base and their needs clearly, it just takes a little imagination to figure out a way to make things better for them and create a business for yourself.

My friend who is an expert in public relations, Phil Lobel, started out as a young entrepreneur in his college days. He shared with me the story of a client with big goals who wasn't ready for the publicity she wanted. By following Phil's coaching, she now is an icon with the TV show *Hoarders*.

Case study: A client of Phil Lobel's, owner and president of Lobeline Communications

Dorothy Breininger was an organizer. She came to Phil 17 years ago, when she didn't even have a press kit. According to Phil, she said, "Oh, I wanna be a professional organizer, a famous professional organizer."

He instructed her that she would need pictures and a press kit, and to put down on paper what she wanted, what her goals were. "Do all that, then come back to me. Then you'll be ready for a publicist, perhaps."

She came back a year later, surprising him by how quickly she accomplished everything on the big-dream list they had discussed. She told him, "Okay, I'm ready for PR, I believe."

He said, "Well, okay, what kind of cases are you working on that might be an interesting news story?"

Dorothy said, "Well, the district attorney's office has asked me to do this thing on a pro bono basis. They wanted to put this guy in jail. It's this hoarder who had a rat infestation, and lice and all this stuff, and his house is just filled with junk. They want me to do a case study to clean up this health hazard to the community."

Phil agreed it was interesting and thought he could get her a lot of press on that. "I see a lot of interest and the potential in this story," he said.

So he reached out to the district attorney's office, knowing they would want to put a friendly face on the office to show they have a nice side. Phil says, "I reached out to the *LA Times* on this story. Long story short, it became a column-one story on the front page of the *LA Times*, two pages on the interior of the *LA Times*, and it got syndicated around the country. The next month Dorothy got an appearance on the *Today Show*. Before we knew it, there was this new offer that came up for this new show they were creating called *Hoarders*, and Dorothy became one of the most famous professional organizers in America."

YOUR INSIGHT Do you see anything in the news or in your community that needs your skills? Is there an opportunity for you to do something publicly that will bring you positive attention, moving you towards your business goals, in the same way Dorothy did?

Investing in your relationships

I still stay in touch with my mentors and find ways to celebrate my former clients. No matter how busy I am with my current work projects, I know that my reputation is my business. How people remember their experiences with me and feel remembered by me is so important. Sometimes referrals come out of the blue from real estate colleagues who saw me speak at a statewide event. Instead of viewing my colleagues as competition, they are my referral sources. Not every client is a good fit for them, so as they know me through events and social media and personally, they can determine if their referral is a good match for me.

I interviewed an agent who was not a good fit for my team and sent him to one of my mentors. And recently, when I needed a new staff member, I did my outreach to my community to see if someone could refer a trusted administrator. In a busy environment, it is useful when we can help each other recruit faster and get our teams lined up with the right talent. No matter what business you are in, it is an important investment to make time for your relationships so you can get the help you need, be there as a supportive colleague, and get repeat business and referrals from your quality contacts. It never is about the one transaction or event, but about the relationship and reputation I build, which is my quality brand.

Wisdom quote from Arturo Villarreal, founder and president, Virtus Building Corporation

Arturo grew up in a big family with a single mother in South Central LA. The family had financial challenges and he started working as a teen to help support the others. His loyalty and character as a teen earned him the respect of mentors, who took him far. In our interview, he still credits the mentors who gave him opportunities and the training that laid the foundation for his company, Virtus. He also credits his team of employees and finds ways to develop his staff so they grow in their skills and stay invested in the company. He personally visits his client sites to make sure each project is going smoothly.

Take care of your relationships

"You can have all the experience in the world, but if you forget to take care of your clients and the people who help make that happen, you have accomplished nothing."

YOUR INSIGHT Do you have a way of taking care of your relationships? If not, create a system to help you manage your clients and network. Think of ways to show you care. Do you need to mail a handwritten thank-you card or drop off a thoughtful gift?

Find your tribe

I have gotten more confident as a speaker and meeting facilitator since I joined my professional networking group. I was in other groups before, but this one has high-caliber lawyers and financial professionals I would not have gotten to meet elsewhere. I have clear affinities with some of my colleagues and we have become friends. We all pay to belong to this networking group, but I hang out with some of these friends in my free time outside meetings. To find your tribe is so important. They can call me out on my habits or weaknesses in a kind way, and I trust they have my best interests at heart. Like me, they are all driven and goal-oriented. So when I have something stressful to discuss, we understand each other well. I am not going to be a legal expert, and through these relationships I can count on being able to find a friend who is a trusted colleague who can either be my professional support or refer me to someone great. You don't have to connect with everyone in a group. There will always be someone who doesn't like you for no obvious reason. You can trust your gut and know who your natural allies are.

Wisdom quotes from Mark Batson, music producer

How to find people to collaborate with

"Find people who excel at things you don't excel at. Understand your strengths and weaknesses and ask how you can offset those weaknesses with other people. Sometimes I find myself around artists who are more extroverted than myself in terms of public persona... More people are going to listen to Eminem rapping to my music than me. It's important to know he has a superstar quality, let me team up with him to get my message across. There are technical and engineer skills that I might not excel at in the studio, and I'm looking for people who are better than me to collaborate with."

YOUR INSIGHT Do a T-diagram with your strengths on the left and your weaknesses on the right. Who in your inner circle or your "board of directors" can help you fill in your weaknesses in the right column?

Being driven is important

"If you find an artist—and they can be the greatest artist in the world— and if they are not as driven to have success, you're going to be dragging them along. You might find an artist who is not as talented and they are twice as driven; they would be better vehicles for you to collaborate with."

YOUR INSIGHT   Is there anyone you collaborate with who doesn't have the same drive as you? Is there someone who is more driven than you who can help you?

Pick people to work with who have the same drive and goals you do

"Working with Dr. Dre, that to me is ideal. He is a person who puts an incredible amount of work in the studio, working every single day. I was his right-hand musician for 10 years. That was great, because I want to create every single day. We wound up writing and creating a lot of music together, because it's a great collaboration."

YOUR INSIGHT   Who has been your best collaborator, and why? Can you find someone like that again?

How to choose your collaborators: "Would I do this for free?"

"Trust your gut. Go with your feeling. Sometimes I say no because I don't think it fits with what I do. Alicia Keys once told me, sometimes when you're thinking about things, you're thinking: 'Would I do this for free?' That stuck with me for a long time, so that I know I'm not running after money. Would I create with this person regardless? With someone like her [Alicia Keys], undeniably yes. Overall, I enjoy being in a room creating with that person."

| YOUR INSIGHT If money wasn't a factor, would you work with certain people? If you can clear your slate with people you would enjoy spending time with regardless of money, then you're focusing on your better collaborators.

Collaboration as creating new relationships

I have found it very beneficial to collaborate with brands that are not in my line of business. These other brands share similar ideologies and visions in terms of customer service, display out-of-the-box thinking, and have a similar client base to mine. Every year, when I put together events, I intentionally think of new collaborations with a high-end hotel or restaurant, a luxury car dealership, or some other luxury service so that we can work on bringing our clienteles together. Creating events involving new collaborations opens up new relationships, new opportunities, and new clients.

For example, an annual event I organize is a panel discussion involving four professionals from different industries. I represent the real estate industry, and the others could be insurance, trust and estates law, and accounting. Clearly, our panel provides value to our personal clients, and at the same time we are also expanding our business outreach to new possible clienteles from the other panelists. These kinds of collaborations are key activities to bring your business new relationships.

Corporate sponsorships and collaborations

Athletic shoe companies like Nike will partner with a star athlete like Michael Jordan to promote their brand. Many athletes, including Olympians, look for corporate sponsorships to help pay for their training and travel. The corporate sponsorship and generous financial support are what gives athletes from the United States an edge in some world competitions. Obtaining resources to get better gear, more coaching time, and access to better facilities is an investment to improve performance.

Sponsorships do not need to be big items or obvious advertisements. Elementary schools will have banners from local businesses showing their support and expressing their congratulations to students winning an award or a regional championship. Instagram dog influencers will proudly wear a bandana and offer a discount code for that dog apparel company. Companies will leverage each other's audiences to build a bigger social media following through raffles and free gift contests if you like and follow their promotional partners. For example, a social media raffle contest led by a dairy-free yogurt company leveraged health-conscious audiences from a granola company, a snack bar company, and a nut-milk company. They appeal to the same kind of niche audience, so these collaborations created attention for partner products. It is a similar marketing algorithm to the recommendations on an e-commerce site that say, "If you like this product, you might like these other items."

From big Hollywood productions to independent films, producers have leveraged corporate sponsors to provide expensive settings like a cruise ship or fancy cars for the actors to use in a scene. These strategies are so lucrative that there are dedicated staff to manage product placement on the corporate side as well as the media production side. Famous movies that feature cars and other products include the James Bond series, Men in Black movies, and the Transformers films.

Apple has deliberately worked with filmmakers such as Jon M. Chu and Lulu Wang to showcase what the new iPhone cameras could do for cinematography. These short films effectively garner attention as the filmmakers challenge themselves to find extreme ways of using the small camera to do things that might not be possible with a bigger camera. Not only are audiences entertained by the short film made with the new product, but we also get behind-the-scenes videos of how the filmmakers worked their magic. The audience reaction of awe and inspiration is exactly what Apple is looking for. People are touched emotionally by the films and interested in buying the newest phone with this aspirational marketing.

Media sponsorships can be more powerful than direct ads, since the products are integrated into the entertainment. Done well, product placements can communicate a positive message to the audience's subconscious. Done badly, product placement disrupts the story and annoys the audience. People want a good story and they don't like to be sold to. My friend David Beebe has turned his filmmaking skills to making exciting stories that promote international brands such as Marriott Hotels. He specializes in "branded entertainment." More about his work can be found in chapter 5, "Personalizing Video."

Match the right collaborators

My job as a referral source is to match personalities and needs. People who are extroverted like to work with other extroverts, and similarly with introverts; and people with common interests or a shared cultural background might match up well. Generally, for my own collaborations, I look at experience as a main criterion: people who have been in their business as long as I have been in mine, or longer. They have a commitment to their business that is long-standing and a reputation in their community. A good friend of mine who has less experience in their industry would make a good entertainment attorney for a new indie musician because the new artist might need someone who is more of a peer and whose legal rates are more affordable. The relatively new attorney might be hungrier for work than a more established attorney would be, and willing to work harder for a start-up musician. If a more experienced musician were looking for representation, I would refer them to a more established entertainment lawyer with a higher rate who might have more levers to push and different ways to strategize for their client.

I had a client, Alizeh, in Malibu who unexpectedly lost her husband. As I was helping her sell her home, a strong emotional connection grew between us. She wanted me to help her find a new home in West Palm Beach, Florida, so she could be near her family, but that is not my professional jurisdiction. I did extra research and reached outside my usual network and my company to find the right personality to help this special client. I remembered I had met a real estate agent named Matthew five years prior at a conference. He was someone who had stayed in touch over newsletters and social media. The way he talked about how he helped his clients demonstrated the emotional connection I was looking for. I knew in my gut that Matthew would be a good match for Alizeh through her fragile emotional transition. Going beyond my usual referral efforts, I flew with her to Florida to introduce her personally to Matthew, because my client had become a family member I cared deeply about. During that introductory lunch, Alizeh reached for my hand and squeezed it. That was her cue that I had found her someone she could trust.

Within weeks, Matthew was able to find Alizeh the perfect home with an ocean view similar to the one she enjoyed in her Malibu life. Alizeh expressed how important the ocean element was in helping her heal from her loss. To this day, she sends me pictures of the ocean, sharing her continued gratitude. It was a team effort, made possible because I found Matthew as the perfect collaborator.

EXERCISES

* What successful partnerships or collaborations have you been part of? What were the qualities that made things go well?

* What partnerships or collaborations were difficult? In the end, did they give you the result you wanted? Why were they difficult? What could have gone better?

* How can you grow your network to find the right collaborators? How can you expand or deepen your friendships so people think of you for referrals and word-of-mouth recommendations?

* How do you organize your contact list of collaborators? I keep notes of where they grew up, where they went to college, their hobbies, marital and family status, what music they listen to. From their musical taste, I get a vibe of their personality. Remembering people's birthdays is important to me, so I try to know this information so I can send them a personalized "Happy Birthday" voice memo, which is part of my unique brand.

11

LIFE'S A PARTY: BUILDING COMMUNITY

Darling, it wouldn't
be a party without you.

ANONYMOUS

Gathering together

WHEN I WAS growing up, my extended family of aunts and uncles and cousins would all descend upon my grandparents' house in Michoacán, Mexico, to spend Christmas together. Those fond memories of me running around playing pranks on my cousins, laughing with family, and seeing everyone together give me a sense of what it is to build a community. I like doing small monthly gatherings at my home, where I invite a handful of people and ask each to bring a friend. These casual events allow me to have one-on-one time with my friends and also get to know their guests on a personal level. I take the time to prepare the appetizers and decorate everything myself. There is an intimacy in having a party in someone's home. It is a way for me to let someone in, to let them know we have a more personal connection than if we were at a big event.

I also like to have the big annual parties that I host at a restaurant, with special decor such as ice sculptures, designed lighting, themed props, and photo booths. My gift bags celebrate local businesses I want to support. Parties create a fun memory, a good time, something that people can remember and that enhances my brand. Maybe they met some new contacts or maybe they were just blown away by my attention to detail with the party decorations. One year I installed a fog machine as part of an enchanted forest theme with the intention of creating a light fog on the floor that would give my guests the impression of walking on a cloud. However, as people walked through it, it filled the room like a thick, foggy San Francisco morning where people cannot see more than a few feet ahead. It was an unexpected flop. Some friends remarked that it made them feel as though we were in a steam room at a gym! When it became clear it was all too much, I ran and turned it off. My friends and I had a good laugh about it.

Why do I throw these monthly and annual parties? They help to celebrate my relationships and give people something to look forward to. I want my clients and colleagues to know I am thinking of them as I invest my efforts in hosting the best party possible. And the party theme is different every year, so they have to come back!

Wisdom quote from Phil Lobel, owner and president of Lobeline Communications

Develop your relationships ahead of time

"Without relationships and alliances, you end up banging your head on the wall. [With relationships and alliances,] you suddenly have a network of people working for your common cause and vision."

YOUR INSIGHT Do you have a network of people who are ready to attend or help you launch your events now? If not, how can you more fully develop your relationships so you have your media and supporters ready?

Word of mouth: The personal touch

Collaborations are not only a way to deepen a relationship with a business or colleague, they are also a powerful foundation for word-of-mouth marketing. An established, trusted source is better than any commercial advertising. Referral marketing is the core of my business. The best compliment from my clients comes when they refer me to new connections, especially when it is a family member or someone in their inner circle.

I met my Australian friend Damon, who is in the luxury car business, 10 years ago at a Porsche event in Los Angeles. I bought my Porsche from him six years ago and have referred clients to him from the start. We genuinely like each other and have similar professional styles. That 10-year relationship suddenly brought me a whole family of clients this year. He referred me to a San Francisco realtor who had clients moving to LA. My Internet presence validated my established career, but it was the personal referral that won me a whole family of clients from this realtor who didn't know me personally. So far, they have bought over $20 million in real estate. It all started with a brother and sister, and then they referred their parents. And then their parents referred their two siblings. This one referral from a luxury car broker connection from 10 years ago could not be expected. My frequent marketing efforts keep me on Damon's radar. This is a relationship of repeated social events over a period of 10 years, and this was his first referral, which I am so grateful for. It was after that first Porsche event that he asked if I wanted to be invited to more events, and that is how we developed our relationship. Show up! Every time I showed up to events with Damon, he saw my interest and commitment to luxury brands.

People are more inclined to believe something when they hear about it from a trusted source. It sticks better than an anonymous broadcast through advertising. That third-party validation is more powerful than if you tried to feed your message to them directly. The strength of your brand depends on you tapping into all the ways you can get your message across and, most importantly, your personal connections.

I am proud of the journey my friend Kyle Chan, a jewelry designer, has been on from the beginning of his efforts with his "Wish" bracelet design to his current success. He wore his first design and had his pocket full of bracelets ready to show anyone who was curious. He was strategically showing up at parties and finding influencers who would wear them and take pictures with him as part of his marketing efforts. Kyle was everywhere, and he had friends at every event. You could say he built his business at parties. Most notably, he built these relationships genuinely and created a community of support that boosted his young business.

Wisdom quotes from Kyle Chan, jewelry designer

Hong Kong–born, LA-based designer Kyle Chan began his business in 2010 inside a Los Angeles hospital room, where his boyfriend was being treated for cancer. While spending so much time at the hospital, he dedicated eight hours a day to making the "Wish" bracelets. Within two years, his designs were being spotted on celebrities including Miley Cyrus and Kyle Richards. Starting from small boutiques that sold on consignment and a stand at a popular flea market, Kyle's work is now being sold worldwide. His designs are regularly seen on A-list celebrities and have been worn in TV and film productions such as *Vanderpump Rules, The Real Housewives of Beverly Hills,* and *La La Land.*

Support other people's brands

"I've always been supportive to other people's brands... I just feel like the traditional way to promote your brand sometimes won't work because it's so in your face. I happen to use my name as my own brand, so I was thinking maybe I can just promote myself and people will talk. When people talk, it works way better... Word of mouth is a very powerful tool."

YOUR INSIGHT When have you used your powers to recommend someone else's brand? How did that make an impact? Can you give people easy phrases to help describe your brand?

Develop genuine friendships so people support you with passion
"There are a few key ingredients to be successful. Obviously, first you have to work hard, second... you need to invest in order to make money. If you don't invest in a person, they're not going to help you. You don't have that friendship.

"If you become their friend, they want to help you. Whenever there's an opportunity, they will remember you and they will post that product with passion. They talk about it and love it. They showcase it. You can see such a big difference when they get paid to post something compared to what they want to advertise because they love you. [You can see] they love your brand, they're your friend. It's totally different. People can feel it. It's not a paid advertisement, like, ah, there's a genuine friendship there. They're supporting each other."

YOUR INSIGHT How can you develop friendships more successfully? How do you inspire people to talk passionately about your products or services?

Be a pioneer

Sometimes the party you are looking for isn't there. Be bold and be a pioneer. Especially if you are representing an underrepresented minority or a consumer niche, you might have to create your own event to showcase your work and your community's work. Particularly in the LGBTQ community, people of different shapes and gender expressions might not find themselves represented in traditional events or parties. As I am writing this book, I have decided I need to give more visibility to the Latino community and also improve my Spanish-speaking ability so I can share my message of entrepreneurship with young people whose first language might be Spanish, or an international audience who would connect better with me if I spoke

Spanish. I know, as part of the LGBTQ community, we need to celebrate some of our underrepresented groups as well. It is so exciting to see a pioneering LGBTQ fashion event here in Los Angeles.

Case study: Nik Kacy, creator of Equality Fashion Week and founder of Nik Kacy Footwear

Nik Kacy is an LA-based fashion designer and entrepreneur who identifies as gender-fluid, queer, and transmasculine. Their footwear brand offers sizes that fit those who want masculine shoes but do not fall within the industry standards in size. They also offer gender-neutral accessories such as belts and utility holster wallets. A designer serving a niche market, Nik Kacy has been featured in mainstream press such as *Forbes* and *Fortune* magazines. Their slogan, "Walk your way," challenges the norm of the shoe industry.

In 2018, they launched Equality Fashion Week (EFW), the first and only premier LGBTQ-focused Fashion Week in Los Angeles, an event with queer and inclusive designers and vendors and over 100 queer, trans, and nonbinary models. Among Nik's many community affiliations, they are on the Trans Inclusion Task Force for the National LGBT Chamber of Commerce. This community leader and entrepreneur takes their genderqueer identity and produces events to showcase others of the underrepresented queer BIPOC and queer and trans community.

YOUR INSIGHT Who in your audience is part of a niche community? Are there metrics in your industry that are not inclusive of that community? Can you provide products that better serve that community?

"From the events I produce, which provide equity for our underrepresented communities, to the designs I create, which are all gender-free, I believe that...creating avenues for people to remove gender from products gives them the opportunity to express themselves authentically without limitations of the gender binary."

YOUR INSIGHT How can you produce events that reflect your values and the change you want to see in the world? How can you showcase your audience in an event or partner with another event to gain visibility for your brand and that audience?

Combine your social time with work time

Some of us work a lot of hours and simply need to combine our social events with our business goals. At my monthly parties—which I hosted pre-pandemic and hope to host again soon—I would always invite a few of my closest friends not only because they are good party guests but also so I can catch up with them and set the friendly vibe of the event. I don't want people acting awkward because they don't know others, and these friends are good at helping newcomers have a good time.

Sometimes your efforts can be informal. At an annual conference that my real estate coach Tom Ferry organizes, there is so much material to learn that I have found it helpful to organize a group of colleagues for an informal debrief at the end of the day in my hotel room. Here, we have a personal space where we can break bread, connect, and discuss highlights and things we might have missed. If it wasn't for this debrief, I might miss some key points because I took a bathroom break from this packed-schedule, multiday event. This end-of-day social event is a mastermind group that gives me different perspectives on the content we learn from this conference. We all look forward to this group learning effort that not only is a networking opportunity but also helps us stir innovation. We are combining friendship building with knowledge building.

Beginning with a business networking group over seven years ago, I have become great friends with someone whose charisma drew me to her. I still distinctly remember the first time I met Evie. She has an unmistakable presence, a warm personality demonstrated with hugs, and she has such a dynamic energy and style. Anytime she enters the room, she is a head-turner who instigates the question, "Who is *she*?" I needed to get to know her right away. Even though she was born in Taiwan and English is not her first language, she has so much poise and grace when she speaks. Our businesses don't overlap and we haven't been able to share referrals. Regardless, our bond is strong as we share our entrepreneurial spirit, and we are excited about similar podcasts, lifestyles, spirituality, and self-improvement courses. My friend Evie is a single mom, a busy and accomplished lawyer, and a philanthropist. Her advice is to bring your friends and fun to your networking and community events.

Case study: Evie Jeang, family lawyer and philanthropist

Evie Jeang, founder and managing partner of Ideal Legal Group, Inc., is also a very active community leader, having won many awards for her work. She is a lawyer who understands firsthand the complexities of international family law. Evie has been published in major news media for her expert opinions in areas of immigration policy, international investors in the United States, international divorce, and international surrogacy.

Vulnerability leads to connection

"True friends and a strong community can carry you through the hard times and carry you far. Finding that community that shares a similar value with you is very important... When you show your vulnerability, in a way, you make people feel more connected to you."

YOUR INSIGHT What type of people can be your community during your hard times? Are there personal stories that show your vulnerability that you're willing to share and that are aligned with your brand?

Tap your friend community

"There's no better way at business networking than being with your friend network... Ask for help when you need it. Ask for advice. It's okay to ask for help."

YOUR INSIGHT What personal interests do you have that might blend with your business-building goals? For example, if you play volleyball with a community group, you could suggest a postgame social if there isn't one already, so you can get to know people better. Think of friends in other cities with whom you may have lost contact and see how you can reconnect and support each other's community groups. Are there friends who can help you brainstorm or troubleshoot a business issue?

Another way to combine community networking with work is through community service projects. It's a common practice to send a company team to do a community service project like beach cleanup or tree planting so people can get to know each other in a different context and have a new way of bonding. It doesn't have to be about work goals. The music festival I feature below is an annual event, and they have found a way to nurture a year-round community. Because of the year-round relationship, when people meet up for the annual festival, there is more of a sense of community and pride than at other once-a-year music events.

Case study: Electric Forest

Electric Forest is a unique "open-source" event in Michigan that focuses on electronic and independent bands, and it is also an experiment in collaboration and community. More than any other music festival, Electric Forest harnesses the creativity and passion of its community members. It's not just the spectacular light sculptures of neon trees or the laser-lit musical performances, it is the community that gathers for an escape into an idyllic forest. While other music festivals have gone mainstream or grown with big-label bands, this event stays committed to indie artists and invites members to stay involved year-round through a community action project called the Wish Machine, which racked up 45,000 volunteer hours and raised $75,000 in donations for community projects in 2018.

YOUR INSIGHT How can you create an experience that allows your audience to stay in touch between events and feel a sense of community?

Share resources to throw a party

If you're just starting out with organizing events, you might need a friend with more experience to help you, or a team of colleagues who have different resources. Someone might have a great connection to a florist, another person might have a patio but doesn't have the food covered, and by combining your skills, your team could organize an unforgettable event. It helps to have a theme or a cause to create a sense of cohesion. With the adjustments of quarantine life, virtual parties have been staged creatively by event planners. A colleague, Shana, a balloon artist, is popular and in demand to create sculptures for events and photo shoots, for live and virtual events. Celebrations need to happen no matter what, whether to help launch a new movie or celebrate a wedding.

My friend Chad Hudson is a successful event planner, and I have seen him grow his business from his early house parties to his current company employing many team members. As he has grown his business from Chad Hudson Events, the bigger part of his business is now for film and TV premieres (like the Twilight Saga) with the top Hollywood studios as well as other corporate events. Especially when he has events involving movies, he brings part of the movie set into the party so that the guests feel they are part of the action, to enhance audience engagement. During the pandemic restructuring of restaurants, Chad was a pioneer in helping his community of restaurateurs stay in business by helping them design attractive outdoor dining spaces. He recently rebranded to CH Cre8ive and his new company has offices in Los Angeles and New York. If you're new to hosting events, Chad recommends you start off organizing smaller gatherings like cocktail parties or a pre-party so you can enjoy early success and then begin to build your brand.

Wisdom quote from Chad Hudson, owner and president, CH Cre8tive/Chad Hudson Events

Your event staff and vendors represent you

"We have a level of sophistication to our events that we try to keep clear throughout... [Your brand is] something you just need to trans-late through all your marketing and through the staff and everybody that you hire that represents you. We make sure everybody is really outgoing and happy and fun, [that] everyone is willing to help out and step in."

YOUR INSIGHT Start collecting colleagues and vendors you can call on if you need to plan an event. Make sure they represent your brand as well.

EXERCISES

- How can you add a community component to your events?

- What type of yearly, monthly, or weekly events do you want to put together that will help you spread your message and vision?

- Who can you collaborate with in throwing a joint event, where you all share a similar clientele?

- Put together an annual event calendar at the end of each calendar year to keep yourself accountable.

- Create a checklist system of what is needed for every event. This will be very helpful for future event planning.

12

NETWORKING AND PHILANTHROPY

You must be genuinely
interested in people.

DALE CARNEGIE

Create a quality network

WITH MY mom's connection to a wholesale source of designer purses and luggage, I earned so much money that I was able to buy my first car as a college student (a Mercedes!), all cash. My mom would not have been able to retail those purses on her own. It was her connections through her clothing business that led us to this wholesaler that supplied us with brands like Louis Vuitton and Gucci. It was my idea to sell this designer merchandise at a markup from the wholesaler's price while offering a competitive discount from regular retail prices. My unique customer base came from the networks I had at the University of Southern California and the senior home facilities managed by my high school friend's family. USC was full of wealthy students who wanted the latest in fashion. The senior homes had a nursing staff who saved up for their luxury treats. Purses were great items to sell because women would see their friend with a new purse and the word-of-mouth referral spread like wildfire. The customer network built itself. And because people were getting a good deal, sometimes they would buy more than one, so they could have one of each color!

I was able to build my real estate practice primarily through the power of networking. Networking was something I learned in my college days at USC. In a marketing class, we were taught the power of relationships and how to leverage those relationships to gain new market share, learn new skills, and obtain new opportunities by helping those around us.

At first, I made the mistake of thinking that successful networking was a numbers game. I used to go to every networking event I could possibly attend, and pass out as many business cards as I could. That was a huge mistake and a waste of time. Building a network is about the *quality* of connections. It's about the amount of time you spend with your colleagues. It's about creating a win-win scenario for each of the people in your sphere. It also comes down to chemistry and personality. At the end of the day, we do business with people we like, people with whom we have things in common.

Building a quality network has a compounding effect if it is done correctly. I have created a weekly networking schedule for myself: three lunches, three coffees, one large networking event, and 20 follow-up calls. The crucial thing in building a network is not to forget about the people you met earlier. The follow-up and relationship building is key. I make it a point to see every person in my database at least once a year. I know that may seem impossible if you have hundreds if not thousands of people in your database, but there are other ways to reach them. For example, you can have a large event every year, or multiple small events. You can also connect with them via social media, which is another way of keeping in touch with someone. I also love sending out handwritten cards every single week. The key is staying top of mind with people who know me and thinking about how I can keep providing value to the people within my network.

I had the good fortune of being mentored by my career counselor at USC, Scott Turner. Even after I graduated USC, he continued to invite me to social events. He is now an independent career coach, so you no longer have to be a student at USC to get his help. I am delighted he shared his wisdom in an interview for this book.

Wisdom quotes from Scott Turner, executive coach

On getting started with networking

"The biggest piece of advice is don't make this too complicated."

"The same underlying techniques apply to everyone, it doesn't matter your industry."

"Start building your network on LinkedIn."

"Get comfortable doing it with people you know before you do it with people you don't know."

"Networking is all about building relationships. The important thing is that it's a 50/50 relationship. You're giving as much as you're taking."

YOUR INSIGHT What can you give when you meet someone new? Notice something about them. Start with a genuine compliment. Ask them what resources they are looking for.

"Most people approach networking as 'I just need to get a job. Get me a job.' That's not what it's all about. That mindset is wrong. You really need to shift your mindset from 'I need a job' to you're exploring your options and you're looking for matches. It's very much like dating. You're going out on dates with people and you're getting a feel for how the relationship is. You're trying to find the best way to communicate and the best way to relate with that person."

YOUR INSIGHT How do you need to shift your mindset? Is it in scarcity mode, and do you need to switch to an abundance mindset? Remember how you feel when you have met a match, some chemistry with a new friend. Journal about that so you can more easily identify those sparks when you are meeting new people.

"Always, always, always, present yourself as a problem solver. 'Is there a problem, or a project that you're working on, that I can help solve for you?'"

YOUR INSIGHT Sometimes people aren't willing to ask for help, so offer! What valuable skills or knowledge are you willing to share with a potential new friend? Offer those skills in a conversation. Is it finding the best restaurant or some hidden hiking trails?

Reach outside your current circle

Not everyone has an entrepreneurial mindset. Your closest friends and family—your inner circle—might want to be protective of you, to prevent you from being disappointed when you don't succeed at first. Your business and your branding take time. Find people who don't know you well, in your middle and outer rings, and who have a similar entrepreneurial mindset. They will be the ones you can go to networking events with, not your friend who is shy and content with their job.

When you're branding your business, it is best to practice with people who don't know you too well. Your parents might still be holding the image of you as a clumsy kid, and your high school best friend may not have caught up with your new, more mature entrepreneur image. It's better to reach out to the middle ring of your social circle and see if someone will be your networking buddy. Quite often, they might know someone at an event to introduce you to. This networking buddy could even be that new friend from the repeated networking events you both attend. Instead of attending independently, you two can plan to meet at a certain time and show up together. In today's connected world, and considering the law of six degrees of separation, you might be able to reach anyone you are looking to meet in only two or three degrees of separation.

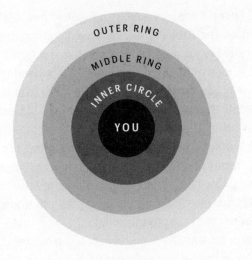

Over a year ago, my entertainment lawyer friend Carla asked me for a referral to a patent and trademark attorney whom she could refer her clients to. Within a couple of weeks of my introducing her to Mo, Carla excitedly called me to share not only that the trademark attorney got rave reviews from her clients but also that Mo had unexpectedly referred several clients to her. His longer career and more extensive network have built more than 20 percent of her new business. Carla was originally interested in matching her clients with the best trademark attorney I knew, but that conversation led to a relationship that has flourished beyond her wildest dreams.

According to Malcolm Gladwell, there are three types of people who can help you with referrals. Aim to meet and develop relationships with all three types, as they will broadcast your brand differently. Also pay attention to what kind of broadcaster you are. There is the Maven, the Connector, and the Salesman. The Maven is an "expert" whose advice people are most likely to follow. They might not be an actual expert on the subject. Mavens have such a strong influence and authoritative reputation for giving reliable referrals that 10 out of 10 people who hear their recommendations will follow through to see that movie or eat at that restaurant. The Connector has many networks, and while they are not as influential as the Maven, they know people in the different industries you might need to contact. A friend who is a "jack-of-all-trades" is most likely a Connector, a bridge to different communities. The Salesman is charismatic and influences people emotionally. They might not have the statistics or specs from Consumer Reports, but their enthusiasm gets you interested in that new tech product they are talking about.

As with most personality-type concepts, you can be a blend of two types. I am an enthusiastic Salesman with a side of Connector who loves to match my colleagues to help them out. You can take a test online to find out what type you are (see the Resources). Be sure to develop relationships with colleagues who will broadcast your branding in their own style to help you build your brand more thoroughly and reach a wider audience.

Join networks that share your philanthropic values

From my very first impression, I was drawn to the aesthetics of Soho House and its focus on supporting creatives. Not only do the people at Soho House build community by offering education programs from cooking classes to filmmaking, they also foster shared values of creativity and philanthropy. My friend Imene introduced me to Soho House, and she is currently on their board. In the early chapter of our friendship, Imene remembered that I gave her a great introduction to Los Angeles when she was new in town, connecting her to people who would help her. Since I am a proud native Angeleno, I showed her how Los Angeles is the place where your dreams can come true. Imene stands out as a giver and philanthropist, and she recruited me to join Soho House because its values match my brand. The network of creatives there reminds me of what my colleague Mark Batson says about creating a winning circle.

Wisdom quote from Mark Batson, music producer

Assess your current network: Like attracts like

"Move in circles of people who have the same dreams and vision that you do. You are the five people who are closest to you. Spend as much creative time, business time especially, dream time, with people who have the same level of ambition, or much more ambition than you do, so you can see where you should be. I'm an optimistic person, and I thrive best around optimistic people who believe their future. I want to be around people who want to be legendary for their art. The phone calls get different. When people are winning, that inspires me. I'm the biggest fan of my friends. Make sure your circle is a highly motivated and ambitious circle of friends so that when they win, that can rub off on you and you can have the same wins like they have."

YOUR INSIGHT Are you around the type of successful people you want to be like? Are there friends who are not supportive? How do you want to improve your network? How can you be more supportive to your successful friends?

Stand out as a giver

Taking the initiative to reach out makes you stand out as a giver. In a context of busy lives and physical distance, it's important to find creative ways to connect. A good friend of mine from high school sends me unexpected small gifts in the mail even though our social lives don't conveniently mix. It's her gesture of staying connected. Because she started this effort of connecting, I also send her unexpected presents. We can't connect with quality time, but we can check in on each other through these little gifts and notes.

At the beginning of quarantine, when everyone was struggling with the adjustment, I wanted to help support my local mom-and-pop businesses and bring some cheer to my clients. There is a dessert bakery and a bagel shop a few blocks away from my home that I visit weekly, and I wanted these businesses to survive the crisis. Taking all the safety precautions, I spent two days driving around with my dog as my delivery assistant to personally drop off gifts as a way to connect while social distancing. Over 100 of my clients got a package of cookies and bagels delivered to their front door. Some people came out to say hi, while others waved from inside. As part of this project, I also took videos in front of these two shops and posted them on social media to advocate for people to come support these shops. In line with my values of supporting local businesses, I am glad to have played a small part in these two shops staying open in my neighborhood.

My colleague José Cabrera stands out as a giver. He is a pioneer as a Latino artist who is also a therapist, specializing in healing trauma and domestic violence. He is also a community leader among his colleagues. He continues his childhood passion of being an artist and is the author of bilingual children's books. We talked about finding fulfillment.

Wisdom quotes from José Cabrera, therapist, artist, and author

Find balance and fulfillment

"It's coming to some balanced approach to this thing called life. How can I give and how can I take? Usually what ends up happening is we start giving more, because that feels more fulfilling, that feels richer."

YOUR INSIGHT What do you need to do for your balanced approach and fulfillment?

Join groups of like-minded people

"Surround yourself with like-minded people who support each other. You've got to be out there and connected. It's not all about making money. It's about giving and joining groups that can really be helpful."

YOUR INSIGHT Do you belong to groups that give you the opportunity to support others? Also consider groups that meet online. Virtual meetings based in other cities can offer you more choices.

Organize a public program

As I build my "Brand With" business, I am offering a number of scholarship students the Brand with Video course so more people will know about this resource and see I am offering accessibility to underserved entrepreneurs. I am also organizing for a significant number of *Brand with Purpose* books to be donated to community groups, where I can reach young people and provide guidance for their entrepreneurial success. As part of my community giving efforts, I will also be doing public speaking events at organizations and schools to expand my mentoring outreach.

My colleague who does branding for small businesses, Liz Marie, offers public programs specifically to help underrepresented women and minority entrepreneurs. She sets up a scholarship program and, through an application, an entrepreneur can receive mentorship and services when their growth might otherwise have been limited because they were unable to hire a professional. These examples of public programs lead us to new networks of people who might not have had the opportunities others have, and they grow the impact of our work. We no longer are limited to our direct networks, but we can build through other organizations' networks.

If you can find a way, donate your services or goods to a bigger cause. It is a way to feel connected to a greater good and find community. You don't have to do it all. Please refer to the previous chapter about community building to see how you can leverage other colleagues and vendors to help you with your philanthropic efforts.

Putting together a fundraiser or networking event usually requires a venue. Restaurants and catering are part of an event, but they don't manage the flowers, the decor, the printed invites. Nobody does everything. However, they are all key partners. If you have a favorite restaurant, go ahead and ask them if they can host your event. If you want their help and they share your vision, you might just make a deal that works for everyone. If you propose a less busy weeknight for an event, you are bringing the restaurant publicity and new customers they would not have had. Find a way to make it a win-win situation for all your team and vendors. Here's an example: because their restaurants are designed to have great event space, the An family has raised money for multiple charities, including those centering on children or tsunami disaster relief in Japan.

Wisdom quotes from Catherine An, restaurateur and philanthropist

Catherine An is a well-loved philanthropist and CEO of An Family restaurants, known for Crustacean, Tiato, and An Catering. She is one of five sisters who help manage their family restaurant empire of Euro-Vietnamese cuisine founded by their mother, Helene, popularly known as "Mama An."

Build charity fundraiser parties as a collaboration

"My clients, they support me a lot. So I want to support them too. We find a goal, or a charity that speaks to both of us. And it's something easy for us to collaborate on and build that synergy around that."

YOUR INSIGHT Do you have an event space you can partner with to put on events? If you don't have all the resources to put together a memorable party, are there ways for you to team up with colleagues to put on an event?

Helping in tough times

"We try to spread it out, we get a lot of requests from different charities to donate food and donate a gift certificate. We rarely ever say no, because they are always good [charities]. Food is something that is essential, and it's always helpful. That's something we could do, we always try to do it. As much as my restaurant was hit hard during COVID, I still try to put a percentage of our budget to the [Los Angeles Regional] Food Bank. I figured, even if it's just one dollar here, a dollar there, it's helping somebody. And I got a lot of satisfaction from personally giving food to the elders, and then to other people in the food industry, knowing how much they need it, and how grateful they are."

> YOUR INSIGHT Especially when times are tough, can you stand out from the crowd and be helpful to an individual or organization?

Every act of kindness counts

I remember how fortunate I have been when mentors like Fran Hughes and Rick Dergan personally offered me help in my journey (see chapter 7, "Building a Team, Expanding Your Brand"). Imagine how many people may not have had the good fortune of finding a mentor! If you can volunteer to be a mentor in a community program, or simply offer services to someone you don't know directly, we can create a ripple effect like a pebble in a pond that reaches farther than your immediate network.

I also remember the scholarship I got from Foresters Financial that helped pay for four years of college. This competitive scholarship had meaning that went beyond just the monetary component. I was inspired by the fact that the judges for the program, people who didn't know me, believed in supporting me in my journey. That scholarship meant they saw the potential in me. My essay shared how important it was to be the first generation of my family to go to college. Beyond my individual achievements, my efforts were a big win for my parents, a result of their sacrifice in immigrating to the United States, leaving behind the comfort of their Mexican homes.

Scholarship and mentoring programs are ways to indirectly show your values and your brand. The goodwill you extend to your community is a warm gesture that supports your reputation. We all love to hear stories about heroes, people taking someone under their wing, the kindness of strangers.

Every act of kindness counts. As so many of us have survived bullying in school and other disadvantages in our upbringing, I was impressed by this effort by IKEA to talk about positivity in a way that might not be a direct sales effort but brings the community together to generate more kindness.

Case study: IKEA's Bully a Plant Project

Seeing a rise in bullying in schools, IKEA wanted to show how positive comments and bullying can alter a plant. In a project commissioned with an ad agency, IKEA brought two plants into a schoolroom for this 30-day experiment. The plants were given the same amount of water, sunlight, and fertilizer as the control; the only explanation for the difference in plant growth was the exposure to recorded compliments or mean comments played on a loop. The goal of the project was to raise awareness about bullying. And you guessed it: the bullied plant withered and the complimented plant thrived. If plants can be hurt by mean comments, humans would be hurt too.

YOUR INSIGHT Is there a community project you would like to organize to extend the goodwill of your brand? How can you engage with your audience in a community service way? If you can't think of how to initiate a project, research what types of projects you might like to join. Name three to five options that are possible to include in your planning for the upcoming year.

EXERCISES

Learn to be approachable. Baby steps: If you're one of the shy people, make an effort in a low-stakes situation, like at the grocery store or when you see someone walking a dog. (Dog people are much more accustomed to random hellos!)

Make eye contact and smile to acknowledge a person's presence. If they look back, you can say a friendly hello, and if it feels right, ask about an item in their grocery cart that you're interested in, or offer a compliment about their dog. You might have the beautiful impact of giving a little joy or a smile to a random stranger.

Sometimes, if you can let someone into the grocery line ahead of you, that is an act of kindness and joy you can both share, especially if they only have a few items and you have a large order to check out. Or if you want to spread the gift of abundance, you could buy a stranger coffee or breakfast.

Find opportunities for random acts of kindness. Practice doing five a week. Practice makes it easier!

Bigger steps: Once you are comfortable making eye contact and saying brief hellos to people, take it to the next level. Start casual conversations and ask people questions that let them tell you who they are—not necessarily about their job, but their interests. If you know someone at an event, make an effort to introduce two people who don't know each other, think of what they might have in common, and help them make a new connection. It could be that they are both wearing a similar shade of blue, or that they both went to school in the same city, or they both love a certain type of music. Whatever people have in common is a great way to start breaking the ice. Wouldn't you want someone to help you break the ice so you can make a new connection?

Grow your social network. Name a few areas of expertise you can share with a nonprofit board or arts committee. For example, if you are a graphic designer, that could be an asset to a community group who needs to work on their marketing and outreach.

- Name a few areas of interest you would like to explore. For example, if you want to get more involved with your ethnic heritage, would you like to join a casual meetup group that watches films in that language? Or do you want something more established, such as a community center that represents that group?

- If you don't know where to get started, tag along with a friend who is more active in the areas you would like to grow. If someone you know goes to a lot of music events, ask them to recruit you for their next outing or send you newsletters or social media channels they subscribe to.

- Name a few people in your network who are more active and social. Do you admire their networking skills? Join them at their next networking or social event. If you don't have friends who are "social butterflies," find an entrepreneurial friend or colleague who has a similar goal of growing their network, and you can be event buddies; you can encourage each other to go meet people but have someone to come back to if you run out of steam.

- Apply to a community program where you work with other people. It could be as low-commitment as a one-time volunteer event packaging groceries for a food bank or planting trees. Try three to five different activities and see what aspects you like and what fits with your values and brand. Keep trying until you find something you might like to pursue in more depth. You gotta do something different to create a different outcome. And if you're open, you'll meet new friends and potential business connections!

Explore your existing social network. Rediscover or deepen connections you may have forgotten about.

Look at your friend list on Facebook, Instagram, or other social media. See who has skills or community connections that you're looking for, make a fresh connection with a comment on their posts, or send a message if there is something you would like to inquire about.

Connect with people you've met through friends but have not yet added to your friend list. Join a new community or interest group.

Update and fill out your LinkedIn profile. This is your professional presence online. Ask friends or colleagues to endorse or verify the skills you've listed. Find people on your other social media that you want to connect to here on your professional network. Connect with your alumni group or choir or any other community group you have participated in. Find topics that you would like to learn more about and join those LinkedIn groups so you can read articles posted by others and comment on them. You might even decide to write an article or share a link to your videos in these topic groups. When you write an article on LinkedIn and share it, you establish yourself as an expert in that topic, and you can repurpose that article to share in your other platforms, such as your newsletters or Twitter.

13

CREATE CONTENT

Take control of the narrative with
your content. Someone has to.

Stories matter

STORIES MATTER and they shape the world, especially for young people. When I was a kid, the only Latinos I saw on television were singers and people in TV *novelas*. Subconsciously, I was told I didn't exist. We need representation to see that a world of possibilities is available, instead of feeling pressured to "fit in." At school, I was made fun of for being different. I so badly wanted to blend in and tell people I was Italian and not Mexican. And even though I didn't know I was gay until later in my teens, I was frequently bullied by other kids who treated me in a nasty way and called me names. Society's prejudices created an underlying fear of being different, which was associated with being mistreated. My family and I worried that if I came out, I would not be offered certain career and life opportunities. In fact, the opposite happened. When I came out loud and proud and started going to LGBTQ business networking events, my business and my confidence grew exponentially. Being publicly more authentic led to spiritual and personal growth, and that attracted clients and business.

In my content now, I know I am reaching younger people, and I want to be the role model I was looking for when I was a kid. I aim to communicate the message that it's okay to be different. And for this book I have intentionally looked at my network to find a diversity of people I could interview to share their wisdom with you. And for those I wasn't able to interview, I've brought in their stories through their various interviews, podcasts, and talks. Through media and the creation of content, we are able to mold what the future looks like and expand what is "allowed." We can spread the notion that everything you want can exist, and that you, no matter how different you are, are included. The power of content can help unite us, and we need to be responsible for the content we put out.

Who are you representing?

I want my content to unite people, to show them they have something more in common than their race, sex, gender, or any other identity. A storyteller I have admired is Greg Berlanti. He is someone who has been honored by the Los Angeles LGBT Center for his impact in the media and is active in the LGBTQ community, and I even had a chance to meet him at a friend's party. He is known for his work on several television series, including *Dawson's Creek, Brothers & Sisters, Everwood, Political Animals, Riverdale, Chilling Adventures of Sabrina,* and *You.* I am so impressed by what he represents, that he seeks to give visibility to gay and trans heroes. He is a pioneer in storytelling and an active part of his community.

Case study: Greg Berlanti, producer, writer, and director

Among his many accomplishments and awards as a prolific TV writer and producer, Greg Berlanti's movie *Love, Simon* stands out. This film featured a gay romantic story, and it is one of Berlanti's many efforts to showcase gay and trans characters. His TV show *Supergirl* cast the first transgender superhero, actor Nicole Maines. Berlanti has cast Ruby Rose as a lesbian superhero in *Batwoman.* With over 20 years' experience and almost 60 projects under his belt, Berlanti's brand is about telling stories of how normal people are superheroes and superheroes are just like us.

Take risks

About being a young showrunner for Dawson's Creek: "Well, if I'm probably going to fail anyway, I might as well fail telling stories that I would want to see."

YOUR INSIGHT Making change is about taking bold risks. What risks can you take in your content?

Stand up for your values

As showrunner of *Dawson's Creek*, Berlanti was responsible for the first same-sex kiss by two men on prime-time network television.

"In the beginning, there was resistance. When we did the Jack kiss on *Dawson's Creek*, everyone was tentative. But I took over the show and that was an important thing to me. If we were going to bring the character out, it seemed silly to me that he couldn't kiss... [If they said no to the kiss,] I was prepared to quit."

YOUR INSIGHT How can you stand up for your values?

On the power of media

"I knew how important TV had been for me as a lifeline. Having been so alone and having felt somewhat connected to certain characters through the television set, I felt like it was a very rewarding part of what could be the storytelling process."

YOUR INSIGHT What form of media is important to you? What is rewarding to you in storytelling?

What world does your content create?

About having LGBTQ *superhero characters:* "What good are these heroes if they don't look like the world they're saving?"

YOUR INSIGHT How does your content create a world you want to serve?

Show the love for your success

"Growing up gay is hardest at times to receive the love that you really deserve. You are your own success story."

YOUR INSIGHT What successes can you celebrate in your content?

Create more opportunity

"As for who's portraying or directing or writing those parts, the primary goal, I think, still needs to be to get more opportunity for the people that have been marginalized. It's better for our storytelling. It's better for the audience. We will have better stories if more people get to share their story."

YOUR INSIGHT How can you create more opportunity to share a diversity of stories in your content?

What content can you create that is unique?

No one sings and performs the way I do. I love incorporating a song into a video or in a voicemail I leave for someone's birthday or on my social media. Choosing to share my other skills helps differentiate me from my colleagues. It helps me stand out and create an emotional memory. People might find me because their friends like a song I sang and shared it around social media. It gives us something in common that we are passionate about. When I sing, I'm sharing my heart in the performance and it makes my video come alive. When people can associate me with something they already love, it's a positive association that gives me visibility and a sweet spot in their memories.

If I chose to be shy and not share my other talents, I would not be presenting the full version of myself. I want to share the joy and laughter of my musical tastes and create an opportunity for my audience to bond with me. I've always been a salesperson, and people choose to do business with me because of my enthusiasm, charisma, and personality. They might not know how a business transaction will go with me if they are a first-time home buyer, but creating content to help people give me their trust is key to a strong relationship.

My friend Anisha started out with her training in law and used that technical background to drive her career where she could influence entertainment content. She noted that after the movie *Legally Blonde* came out, there was a spike in women enrolling in law schools across the country. It showed the influence that media can have in shaping social trends. If more underrepresented people see new possibilities for themselves through entertainment and media, it will open up ideas for career paths they might not see reflected in their community.

Wisdom quote from Anisha Manchanda, VP of development and production at Content Superba

Anisha is an Indian American who grew up in Dubai and the United Kingdom. Her international background gives her an eye for international content, and she has a personal mission for diverse talent and inclusive storytelling. She began her career as an attorney at an investment bank in the United Kingdom. As an entertainment lawyer in Los Angeles, she has worked at CAA and Hutch Parker. Projects she has been involved with include *Logan*, *X-Men: Days of Future Past*, *Paper Ghosts*, and *Slay*.

Why producing content is so powerful

"I want to tell stories that haven't been told… The biggest thing we talk about is having an emotional connection that's going to resonate with the audience… It starts with a really great story always. But then beyond that, from recognizing a book or an article and to actually putting it out on the screen, there are so many people involved. That's why the interesting job of the producer is so fun. You get to marry all those components."

YOUR INSIGHT If you want to have an influence on the stories being told, what role and situation can you be in to give yourself that influence? There are many possibilities: create a comic strip, join a street mural team, produce a podcast, or help someone else tell the stories. If you don't have the resources to produce your own content, can you be a guest speaker on someone else's podcast or production?

Sharing the power

If you already have a way of creating content, can you do it differently? I was creating video for my real estate brand, but I wanted to create a series for inspiration and motivation. A few years ago I made the first episode of *Breaking the Chain* to highlight bold entrepreneurs. It wasn't the right time for that series to get developed, but it was an effort to expose my existing audience to more ideas. Whenever I put on events and have a chance to promote my colleagues, I recruit their business cards to put in the swag bag or buy their products to share with my audience. Padma Lakshmi has gained power as a TV host and producer and has chosen to share her audience to expose them to new ideas.

Case study: Padma Lakshmi, author, actor, and TV producer of *Taste the Nation*

As a successful model, actor, author, and businessperson, Padma Lakshmi has used her influence to create a show, *Taste the Nation*, that puts the spotlight on the diverse food cultures of immigrant and Indigenous communities. Well-known as a host on *The View* and as a producer and judge on *Top Chef*, she uses her producer power to reflect her values as an activist. She is humble about her shortcomings and generous in creating a space to invite people to share their stories in their own words. As an immigrant herself, she offers a perspective into communities that is not the same as the escapist point of view of most mainstream food shows. She gives background to the complicated and sometimes oppressive history that has shaped ethnic cuisine in the United States. This honesty brings unusual content to a TV series about the diverse food history of the United States.

Pass the mic

"This is my rebuttal to the fear-mongering [about immigrants] from Washington… The whole point was to give the microphone to the people responsible for the most exciting food in the country."

YOUR INSIGHT How can you use your influence or platform to give the microphone to other people? How can that choice be unique and exciting and enhance your brand?

What is your intention for your impact?

"I designed this show not for people who think like me, not people who are necessarily gung-ho about immigration policy, but for people who are against it. This country is mighty because of its immigrant labor. It has been refreshed and renewed over generations, culturally, economically, because of the influx of different waves of immigration. And that's important to note… I wanted to show that immigrants are not people you should be threatened by. They're not dirty, nothing. And you know that, because you order takeout from them all the time."

YOUR INSIGHT This leader is using her show to reflect her values. What kind of social impact do you want to have with your work, your content?

Where is the action for your industry?

"If you ask me, just from a hard-nosed business point of view, ethnic food in this country is where the action is at. That is what makes American food dynamic."

YOUR INSIGHT What is the cutting edge for your industry? Where is the innovation or cross-pollination happening for your business? Where can you learn from other schools of thought, or from other cultures?

EXERCISES

- What companies or leaders do you admire? What kind of messaging or themes do they have to create their content?

- Are there certain videos or podcasts you especially like? What is their format? Use your favorites to inspire your own brainstorm about the content you would like to create.

- What format of content do you excel at? If you're interested in expanding into a certain area, can you find a team to help you get started in that kind of production?

14

PIVOTING

Your brand doesn't get
better by chance,
it gets better by change.

JIM ROHN

Memories to modernizing

TO THIS DAY, my family and I still pull out albums of childhood photos. These albums have endured the test of time and these printed photos mean so much to us. I have fond memories of my extensive photo shoots, then waiting eagerly for the three days it took for photo developing. The excitement and anticipation we shared when we opened the envelope to see how the photos came out, that is our shared memory. It was the whole experience—taking the photos, admiring the printed photos, and creating the album that we now cherish years later.

Even though the world has mostly gone to digital photography, there is something wonderful about the tactile experience of a printed photo. At events and parties, people who have never used a film camera still enjoy the photo booths that use digital cameras and printers to re-create the fun and nostalgia. Those four photos on a strip of paper are a beautiful souvenir from the event, capturing the joy of you and your friends. My personal fondness for beautiful photographs and souvenirs is why I want to highlight the company Kodak and its history of diversification and pivoting.

Case study: Kodak

Kodak was the pioneer in capturing photographic memories and creating film for Hollywood movies. Since its founding in the 1880s, the company has survived technological changes by diversifying its business. Having been a specialist with chemicals, Kodak made an attempt to grow into pharmaceuticals by buying Sterling Drug in 1988. By the 1990s, though, it sold off the Sterling pharma business for cash to concentrate on its core photographic and imaging business. Even though photographic film has been largely replaced by digital media, Kodak has endured through time by selling off licensing and its patents. The company filed for bankruptcy in 2012. By 2014, it was the only major producer of film for motion pictures. Most recently, in July 2020, it secured a $765 million government loan to launch a new division of Kodak Pharmaceuticals, which will produce active ingredients for generic medications in the United States. It remains to be seen whether they can successfully pivot to this sector.

YOUR INSIGHT Would you like to diversify or to focus on your core specialties? What would help you make a more successful pivot if you want to change your business? Are there strategic partners you need to negotiate with so that you can be more successful in your new ventures?

From the Kodak story, you can see that they failed to stick to pharmaceuticals when they were seeking to grow their company before. It will be curious to see how they can try again in pharmaceuticals and if they will have a different outcome this time. We have to risk failure in order to grow. And a piece of wisdom from some small business and microfinance lenders is: they prefer to give loans to entrepreneurs who have already failed at least once, because that means they gained some experience and are likely to do better the next time.

When technology changes your industry

Technology is changing faster than ever. One of my friends, Mark Batson, is in the music business, an industry that has been affected by tremendous growth in the way music can be made. Hollywood used to have big orchestras that were used to produce the film soundtracks, but now that has changed drastically. The options of using sound banks instead of acoustic instruments and having home sound studios have shifted the way music is produced. Technology has changed the music industry very quickly and fundamentally in the course of Batson's long career; there are shifting metrics as to what makes a hit song, and audiences have largely switched their buying behavior from physical CDs and records to digital media.

Wisdom quotes from Mark Batson, music producer

Everyone has their own lane

"Stay true and fine-tune what I do. Use the technology, keep abreast to it, but don't be a slave to it. What I do the best: I'm a pianist who can rap. I know that those are two things I do well. That's the thing that makes me different and special to other people. There are people who program trap beats and sonics. What I do doesn't come in a box. My creativity comes from my heart and soul. Even as technology is advancing, be aware of what you do, and how you can combine that with technology rather than chasing after the technology. How do I utilize the things that I do better than other people? Make sure I maximize that."

YOUR INSIGHT What is it that you do best, something that other people might not do? How can you keep that specialty at the forefront of your work?

Avoid situations that waste time

"'Avoid situations that waste time'—that's one of my first things I learned as a musician, from a great musician [advising me] when I was younger, playing a gig. You see when things are going nowhere, and you want to avoid those things that are going nowhere and stay with the things that are progressing forward. I've heard that told to me in different ways."

YOUR INSIGHT   Are there people you work with who don't add to your positive progress? Who can you find or spend more time with to help you advance and progress forward? For example, if you're not the fastest to learn technology, can you find someone to team up with to advance your projects?

When you mature and adjust your brand

When I started my real estate career, I was working in a partnership. When I switched to launch my new independent brand, my friend Alek introduced me to expert producer David Beebe, who guided me through this pivot process by helping me shape my new identity. David saw my strengths and gave me confidence to create new content that highlighted my unique value to the real estate industry. David's advice was the reason I created the *Real Estate Minute* series on YouTube, something short and catchy. His affirmative support pushed me through the insecurities I experienced during this life-changing pivot. Learn more about David Beebe in chapter 5, "Personalizing Video."

Wisdom quote from David Beebe, brand storyteller and producer

Learn by doing it

"Whether it's pivoting or trying something new... it's important to have a goal, what you want to accomplish at the end. But you don't have to have everything filled in in between. So it's doing it and learning versus trying to make perfection out the door. It's just not going to happen. You're going to learn from actually doing it. The biggest thing is stop talking about it and start doing it, because... the best way to learn is to try something new."

YOUR INSIGHT How can you let go of perfection, and learn by doing your new thing for your brand?

Another creative leader I interviewed shared her point of view about her brand: Belinda Carlisle, lead singer of the band the Go-Go's, one of the first chart-topping all-girl bands who wrote their own songs, inducted into the Rock and Roll Hall of Fame in 2021. Her son Duke and I are friends, and I have admired how her long music career has her personal stamp on it. She talked about the difference between the band and her personal brand, and the through line is her point of view as a contrarian punk rocker. As she has matured in her long career, she is more protective of her brand and makes certain choices to stay true to her values.

Wisdom quotes from Belinda Carlisle, singer, musician, and author

Protect your brand

"There are choices that I make to protect it. My brand would be more adult… So there are things that I do and won't do. I used to take everything that came my way. Now, protecting my brand, there are certain shows I won't do; certain kinds of certain things I won't do as far as my career goes. [A brand], it's a valuable asset. I may not look like a punk rocker, but I have a punk rock heart. I was born contrary."

YOUR INSIGHT If you're maturing in your career, what essence of your brand do you want to maintain so your audience can recognize your message?

You are more than what you do

"I always thought there was something bigger than myself. And when I turned 40, I was dropped by my record company, for a lot of different reasons. I know that I'm not defined by what I do. I gotta find out who I am. So I started digging deep, reading all these books on finding yourself… When I got sober, I knew I needed all the extra help I could get. I got very much into kundalini yoga, which is my daily practice today, which includes breath work, yoga, chanting… So now I have a very, very solid foundation that I live my life from."

YOUR INSIGHT Can you redefine yourself, separate from what you do? If you need help, what daily practice can you do to give yourself the support you need?

Adapting in a public health crisis

So many of my business meetings used to be held in person at restaurants. As my meetings went to virtual conferencing and phone calls, I had to find ways of making a personal connection, by sending handwritten notes and packages. I missed some of my favorite restaurants and hope they will stay in business after the public health crisis.

Restaurants were among the hardest-hit businesses during the COVID-19 restrictions. Those that persisted used several strategies. As outdoor seating became the new way to offer service, restaurants expanded their outdoor options by taking over parking lots and sidewalks, and even set up tables in lots or on sidewalks that were several storefronts away from their business. Cities such as Beverly Hills and West Hollywood supported their businesses by setting up street blockades to transform parking spaces into expanded sidewalk seating. My colleague Catherine An, managing partner of a restaurant group, describes how she envisioned new ways of adjusting her business model to better serve her customers. While many restaurants closed due to the challenges of pandemic restrictions, Catherine, founder and managing partner of An Catering and Tiato, has chosen imaginative ways to pivot and reinvent the family business to serve the new environment.

Wisdom quotes from Catherine An, restaurateur and philanthropist

Trust your gut and discern what advice to take

"I feel very confident that when all this is over, I'm going to look back and say I'm so glad I listened to my gut and didn't take other people's opinion. Sometimes it's hard, especially when it comes from people you respect. But they're not in the day-to-day trenches that I am in. I know it comes from a good place. I think you also have to be careful when you do take their advice. Weigh out your own options and really figure out what are the risks."

YOUR INSIGHT What can you do to trust your gut better? Whose advice is supportive and whose advice do you need to put to the side?

Ask for help

"Don't be so fearful of how you're perceived. Go within yourself and ask yourself what you really need help on... Don't be embarrassed to ask for help, because that's the only way you're going to get better."

YOUR INSIGHT What are you embarrassed to ask for help on? Is there a way to find a more supportive person you can trust with your vulnerability?

How can you push yourself and come up with creative ways to pivot?

"I can either close down and just see it [the pandemic closures] as a forgotten year, or I can really push myself physically, emotionally, try to learn as much as I possibly can to be able to take my business to a new level."

About Tiato in Santa Monica: "Before, we targeted mainly corporate offices. That was what was in our surroundings, but [now] they all work remotely, and no one's around. I felt like I was starting a new business. It's slowly paying off, because we have such a large outdoor dining space, it would be a shame not to open for dinner. For the first time, I opened up a garden nights dinner service, which I never did before, because I didn't have to. And now we're also doing weekend brunch. Also, I started doing prepared meal services, where people can get our food where it's already prepared for them, but it's delivered to them cold. All they have to do is either put it in the oven or put it in the microwave. It's made easy. Everything is prepped, marinated, and ready. Those are three new revenue streams that I didn't have before that I have now. I make as much money as I did before [the pandemic]... It's going to make us more successful."

YOUR INSIGHT What can you do that no one else is doing? What can you do that you have not done before for your business? What is unique about your business that you can showcase or explore to create a new product?

Other strategies that restaurants adopted focused on expanding revenue streams by selling to-go items such as special "family meal kits," packaging "party packs" that included alcohol and drink mixers, or taking on themes or weekly specials as their menu. As more people were switching to home cooking, the lower volume of regular menu sales led some restaurants to support their produce vendors by selling produce boxes direct to customers, to keep the supply chain going. Some businesses created different marketing strategies, pushing "to-go" orders to engage their customer base.

Small businesses that had previously sold only specialty items expanded their offerings to include essential products such as toilet paper, hand sanitizer, and masks. To stay relevant, clothing companies and fashion designers offered their own versions of the pandemic mask. Service-oriented businesses started selling products. Some businesses shut down completely, while others pivoted and tried different ways of operating in the new climate.

My favorite morning ritual was going to the gym, and during the Los Angeles pandemic closures this became a missing part of my routine. I was delighted when my fitness center was able to pivot and open up on the rooftop of a parking structure. They installed canopies, Astroturf, and rubber mats to re-create the gym environment. Even though it was only 20 percent of their usual equipment, it was safely spaced out and everyone was so excited to be there. There was an app to reserve a 90-minute workout spot in advance. I noticed that the people who showed up in this limited gym setup were also high-performers in their work, as fitness was a pillar of their mental clarity and drive. When times are tough, the effort to pivot and persevere shows the adaptability of a business and creative visioning by leaders.

When life events happen

Some of us have an entrepreneurial spirit that is kept under wraps out of fear. For me, it was only when I got let go from my CPA job that I took the leap to become an entrepreneur in real estate. Losing my job was just part of the accounting company's structural change, but in the moment it felt as though it was an event that was not in my control. However, it turned out to be a gift in disguise, and luckily, I had saved some money before it happened. No matter what kind of work I did, I always brought my work ethic, enthusiasm, and eagerness to learn to every part of my job. That is how my mentors and clients knew me and my brand.

Others start a business because their old job no longer works for their new lifestyle. Sometimes, when parents take time off to have kids, it is hard for them to go back to their previous full-time job when they need the flexibility to juggle work and child care. Sometimes starting a new business is a matter of transferring your job skills to become a consultant in the same field. And as a consultant, you still have to create a brand and market yourself to get new clients. And if you get too much work, you might have to build a team!

My friend Vincent Jones chose to start a new business when he was recovering from a bad car accident. He needed something that was more flexible to accommodate his rehabilitation schedule. The car accident also made him question whether he was really living his dream career. In this pivot, he took his personal brand and audience from his previous work and brought it to his travel business. Do you have dreams you have hesitated about that you want to choose now, or at least plan for? In my interview with Vincent, I asked him what advice he would give his younger self and younger entrepreneurs.

Wisdom quotes from Vincent Jones, social entrepreneur, change agent, and CEO of Citizen Jones Travel

Take risks earlier

"I was always entrepreneurial. But I was afraid to take a leap and better myself. I wish I would have been less risk averse younger... I went to a predominantly white high school and I ran for student class president and won. My mom didn't tell me, but she was afraid I was going to be heartbroken because she thought, 'Those white folks [aren't] going to vote for him.' But I ended up winning by a three-to-one ratio. I was fearless at that point, but for some reason I didn't know I could pursue something entrepreneurial. I wish I would have made that jump earlier to entrepreneurship."

YOUR INSIGHT What have you wanted to do but hesitated on? Are there ideas from your younger years that you possibly want to launch now? Write about those ideas and see where they take you.

Reach out to people you admire

"Find 5 to 10 people who you admire and write to them. Not an email, write them an actual letter. Be very specific about what you admire about them, something that you're thinking about, and why you would be appreciative of a half-hour phone call or Zoom call. People love to be told that they are inspirational. It's about getting advice."

YOUR INSIGHT Name five people you admire. What would you ask them or discuss with them in a 30-minute informational interview? Now, write and send them a letter to schedule that interview.

On pivoting: Every day, you have to recommit to pivoting

"Once you make a decision, you're constantly making decisions. It's like coming out. You don't just come out for one day. Whenever you meet somebody new, you're coming out. Every day, you have to recommit to the idea of pivoting."

YOUR INSIGHT What new branding idea can you write down and expand? If there are opportunities for this, how would you implement it?

On branding: Be obsessive about your audience

"Know who they are, what they do, what they eat, what kind of flowers do they like, where do they vacation, whatever kind of detail about them, you have to be obsessive about it. The details are what makes your brand feel real. Get your audience to say that they are not only going to buy more of your stuff but [they will] tell people about it and [encourage them to] buy it too."

YOUR INSIGHT Is your audience actively engaged with you? Can you imagine a campaign where you do a call to action and incentivize your audience to share their enthusiasm and bring you more fans?

What's in a name and pivoting?

When branding your company, does it make sense to have your personal name in the brand? There is no right or wrong answer; it depends on your goals. From the beginning of my real estate career I chose to have my company name include my name. When people see Ivan Estrada Properties, they can connect my videos and branding to me, no matter where I set up my offices with a larger real estate brokerage. My personality drives my company. My clients know I am the leader of my team. My name helps me get requested to speak at conferences and professional events. As I grow my speaking career and coaching work, it is good for people to see everything I do, to see I offer many services to uplift people's life experiences.

Other entrepreneurs want the world to see their company for a purpose or value that is not tied to their personal name. They choose to develop their branding differently. My colleague Arturo Villareal created his construction company with the name Virtus Building Corporation because he specifically wanted his branding to communicate to his clients the meaning of "virtus": valor, excellence, courage, character, and worth. It was a name that came to him at 3 a.m. after a trip to Rome. He also wanted his company to be much more than him as an individual. He sees his employees as part of his work family that he is responsible for, and he wants them to take pride in the company. As he grows his company, he is mentoring leaders among his employees to help him run the company, so that it could run without him. As he expands his business to include more project management work beyond direct construction clients, the company brand of values continues to flow to the management clients.

My friend who pivoted and now curates travel experiences, Vincent Jones, is known for his taste and style as well as his political and activist point of view. By keeping his own name in the name of his travel company, Citizen Jones Travel, he is sharing his personality and bringing his previous audience to his new company. During our interview, he recommended that we look at the story of an accomplished performer, DJ and trans activist Lina Bradford, who used variations of her name in her career.

Case study: Girlina to DJ Lina

Lina Bradford has shifted from her early career as a dancer, actor, and performer known as Girlina, a name her grandmother called her. Early on, Lina's family was supportive of her transgender identity. Maintaining her iconic New York nightlife persona, Girlina rebranded herself as DJ Lina, becoming known worldwide. DJ Lina is involved in activism as a trans and queer mentor and spokesperson.

Keep the message throughout

"I'm from the school that teaches how every artist has a story to tell. As DJs, we're all on a journey, and it's our job to share it with the crowd from the first song to the last."

YOUR INSIGHT If you're pivoting, are you staying true to your story? How?

Love what you do

"My mother and my grandmother always instilled in me, 'if you do not love what you're doing then you're not living.'"

YOUR INSIGHT Do you love what you do now? If not, how can you pivot to make it more your passion?

Keep open to relationships with kindness

"When you least expect it, there's the relationship that is supposed to be in your life. When you close yourself down, you're blocking the blessing... Talk nicely to people. Don't give shade and attitude. That's not what being fierce is. And you don't need to tell somebody you're fierce if you're fierce."

YOUR INSIGHT Can you think of people who have randomly come into your life and given you gifts? When was the last time you were nice to a stranger? Write down your commitment to random acts of kindness. How can you do them more frequently, maybe five times a week?

Planning for change

Change will happen, and you need to plan for it. You need to become indispensable, and that is through self-initiated education, learning through mentorship, and risk taking (see chapters 2 and 3, "Be Bold and Different" and "Authenticity"). Assess your strengths and find out how you are most valuable to your colleagues and clients (see chapter 7, "Building a Team, Expanding Your Brand").

In order to be most valuable for my business, I have been challenged with learning how to be a better leader as I grow my business and expand my team. As a driver, I have had to learn new managerial styles with my team, working with people who might have different learning styles. With new people on my team, I need to remember how I felt when I was new to the business 12 years ago. I also need to ask my new team members how they feel about their challenges. I have certain advantages and blind spots that my team members don't have. Learning to listen actively, I ask questions like:

- How can I motivate you?
- What do you most like about the business?
- Where are you having challenges? Why do you think you have those challenges?
- What can I do to help with your challenges and help you problem-solve?

To develop a strong team and retain them for the long term, my job is to provide my team with something they can't get anywhere else. Our Monday check-in establishes plans and goals for the week, and on Fridays we have a team "lunch and learn." Not every member can afford the coaches I invest in, so I pass on the tools and lessons I learn from my coaches. I'm not just teaching them how to fish, I also equip them with the tools so they can go fishing on their own. We have each other's back. I ask my members to tell me if there is something I'm not doing, something I can help them with. No matter how busy I am, I need to set aside my priorities to invest in my team members. I see them also as clients, demonstrating to them how I treat clients.

Because I like to focus on staying positive, I struggled greatly with giving performance reviews or delivering bad news to my team. But people who are serious about their career want to know how they can improve. It took me going to a conference to help me change my mindset so I could better grow my team. The speaker I heard in that conference shared how she was hurting her team when she didn't give her colleagues honest feedback. I was able to hear her story and put myself in her shoes to see how it related to my struggle. When I came back from the conference, I started to ask my team members for permission to give them feedback with the intention of helping them improve. Examine what is holding you back from your next important change. The mindset needs to pivot first before anything else can follow.

Relationships and experience are a big part of any business. Some successful older real estate colleagues who are excellent with relationships recognize that they lack marketing efforts with technology. Pivoting and adjusting to new technology means they intentionally hire younger team members who are more aware of social media marketing, trends, and technology so their team can be competitive and up-to-date. I personally use technology to strengthen my relationships and scale my business. Technology can't replace the human experience, and yet it is needed as part of the multiple forms of communication to enhance relationships. Somehow, we need to create memories for our clients so that we can stand out from the noise and competition—the old-fashioned handwritten note, a personalized happy birthday voicemail, or an unexpected gift of appreciation. Leveraging everyone's different skills with relationship building *and* technology is a way for my business to provide a high-quality experience.

Being thoughtful about assessing one's strengths and weaknesses is key to staying relevant and planning for the future. A good example is Wayfair, which recognizes that the home furnishings decor consumer rarely buys furnishings for an empty home. Most consumers buy furniture to add to an existing room. Wayfair understands that consumers need help to see how a product will fit in their actual living space. Wayfair has developed technology and marketing to help take away the hesitation so the customer can feel more confidence in their shopping experience. They have devoted resources to plan and develop for the user experience five years ahead, becoming a leader in future-proofing.

Case study: Wayfair and future-proofing

The founders of Wayfair started in 2002 with product-specific sites and thought about their long-term growth to develop a furniture and home goods destination site branded as Wayfair. They have had 50 percent year-over-year compound growth since 2014. Projections show Wayfair will be selling $112 billion per year by 2030. They have spin-off sites to help people find the styles they want. Wayfair founders view the company as a technology firm and not a home goods retailer, so they employ 3,000 engineers and data scientists to develop their technological platform. They also have a dedicated research and development team to future-proof their business by visioning the technology for the next 5 to 10 years. Wayfair has started a nonprofit consortium with their competitors to develop 3-D technology that will help shoppers visualize their products in their home, similar to 3-D modeling already being used by architects and realtors. Instead of waiting for technology to change the shopping experience, they are proactively harnessing technology to direct the future of their business.

YOUR INSIGHT How do you think your business will have changed 5 or 10 years from now? How can you position yourself to be ready for that? Where can you seek out leading-edge information so you can plan accordingly? What small steps can you take to break out and get to that point? How can you be more adaptable?

YOUR INSIGHT Do you need inspiration from others who have learned to pivot? Look to other stories or test your new ideas with a focus group to validate that your efforts are worth it.

EXERCISES

- If you're afraid of a certain change that needs to happen with your career or business, let's do an inventory. Make a list of what is holding you back, your fears. Then write a list of what you will miss out on if you don't make that change. Look at your opportunities versus your fears. Then find someone to help you take the next step towards your goals. If you don't know who that someone is, ask your network!

- Take two pieces of blank paper. Draw a mind map of your current and previous brands and draw a mind map of your new brand five years from now. What similarities already exist? Are there qualities from your brand you would like to bring forward to your new brand? Are there qualities you want to highlight?

- Who among your audience would transition to your new brand? How can you give them a call to action to join the audience of your new venture?

- Visualize five years from now. How do you see your company growing? How will it need to pivot? What can you carry forward from your current branding, and what new audiences will you need to adapt to for that future company? How can you stay ahead of that growth and prepare for it now?

REFLECTIONS

Don't worry, son. One day, you're
gonna have a lot of pairs of shoes.

MY MOM

Walk a mile in my shoes

WAS CLEANING out my closet recently and found that old pair
of shoes, the ones with the hole in the bottom repaired with duct
tape. I have so many shoes, probably 60 pairs in my closet, that I
had forgotten I even kept them. These dress shoes with the duct
tape on the bottom of one sole were the only shoes I wore for my real
estate work when I was trying to get my career started. Seeing them
for the first time in years took me on an emotional whirlwind—it
made me remember where I started.

When I was working as a caterer to make ends meet and also starting in real estate, I had only two pairs of shoes: a pair of running shoes
and these black work shoes. At that time, I could not afford more. It

was either pay my phone bill or buy a new pair of shoes; I couldn't do both. Even though I wore out my work shoes on both jobs, I always made sure that the tops of the shoes were polished, black, and shiny. These were the shoes I would wear when I walked miles to door-knock at homes. In real estate, I was always door-knocking, and then, as a caterer, I was on my feet zipping from one table to another.

I put so many thousands of steps into those shoes that I created a hole in the bottom of them. I remember needing to make that duct tape repair and feeling sorry for myself. I was so embarrassed about the hole, I didn't even tell my partner, whom I was living with.

This is the story of how one person changed my life and how I will never forget where I came from. All it took was one major client giving me a listing to get me out of my economic tough times. I remember sitting in her living room and talking about the proposed transaction, which was yet to be processed. And then I crossed my legs, revealing the duct tape on the bottom of my shoe. I was instantly embarrassed and felt a pit open up in my stomach, but it was too late. She saw the duct tape, and then she looked at me. I'm not sure if she felt sorry for me or what her look meant, but that was the moment she confirmed her contract with me. It was the biggest transaction of my career up to that point, and it gave me a year's worth of salary. Maybe this deal happened because she saw the shoe and realized how hard-working I was. Her deal was the turning point at the start of my career, when I could finally quit the catering job and just focus on my passion career of real estate.

This story shows how important it is for all of us, in whatever career we go into, as an entrepreneur or not, to remember where we came from—that every little thing matters, from keeping those shoes polished to doing your best to work with pride. The butterfly effect, this one action of one client, changed my circumstances single-handedly. She enabled me to focus on my real estate career. To show my gratitude, I have put this pair of shoes in my entryway, so that every time I leave my home and every time I walk back in, I have a reminder of my journey. I can keep myself humble and never forget.

Humble memories

As I interviewed my experts for this book, I often asked them what they would like to remind their future selves about who they are. These shoes are a blast from the past, and I want my future self to remember my humble beginnings in my real estate career. So I thought I should answer my own question: What would I want my future self to remember?

If you had to evacuate due to wildfires or go on a space odyssey, what would you bring with you? I gave some thought to what I would keep safe in a time capsule. This is an excellent way to do a life review and see what is important to you.

So, here is my list of what I would put in my time capsule and the meaning behind each item:

- *The shoes with the duct tape*
  They remind me to be humble and grateful.

- *My grandfather's watch*
  He believed in my success early on.

- *A photo of my parents and sister and her wife, where we looked so happy at Christmas*
  This was a family moment right after my sister got married. I didn't think it would be possible that my parents would be okay with having two gay kids.

- *A photo of my extended family of 50+ aunts and uncles and cousins on the beach in Mexico at a 2019 family reunion*
  This photo reminds me of how much love we have in our extended family.

- *An old microphone from my uncle who was also a singer*
  He believed in my dream of being a singer when I was 12.

- *A photo of me in eighth grade*
  It reminds me that I have been transformed from the ugly duckling who felt alone in the world, without friends.

- *My memory book of my school years: preschool to high school*
  Every year, my sister and I each filled out our memory book. It is filled with photos, report cards, awards, and drawings.

- *A photo of my dog Noah, who has been with me through so much over the last eight years*
  Whenever I cried during my tough times, he would comfort me. He's been my copilot.

- *This book,* Brand with Purpose
  My important life stories and the wisdom of my community are here.

Who I was—that is the foundation of who I will become. Each day we are becoming, and sometimes it is simply remembering who you are. And for us to remember, we need to be present and mindful of what we are doing each day. It's not just the physical things or the memories in the time capsule, but the meaning behind them. They remind us of the essence of who we are and what makes us happy and grateful.

Journeys

This book has been an intense and personally transformative journey. When I began writing it, I was motivated by a desire to establish credibility to grow as a public speaker. Truly, I ended up growing in many ways as a person, to develop this book more fully and to be of better service to you.

As I went through the process of interviewing my community and asking the questions that would help you, my readers, I realized what we might have in common. I was a kid who didn't fit in, I was bullied, and I didn't see successful, influential entrepreneurs in my community who looked like me. There were singers like Ricky Martin, Shakira, and J.Lo, and that is why I first took the path to singing, since that is what I saw as success on TV. There are many inspirational business books and motivational speakers, but they are not from a Latino or LGBTQ background, and I want this book to bridge the gap for my readers who might not have obvious or famous leaders in their community. I want my nephew to grow up seeing successful leaders who come from all backgrounds. Your success is part of my nephew's future. I made the effort to interview and highlight a diversity of leaders so that you could see the beautiful tapestry of what is possible and you could feel included.

At first, I did not want this book to be "too gay" or to include my story of choosing sobriety. But I realized that I had to walk the walk and follow my own advice. For me to practice authenticity, I needed to share with you my difficult challenges and how I grew through them. In order to ask you to be courageous, I had to be courageous and face my own fears. I had to believe that I was enough, and that my vulnerabilities were also my strengths.

And then came the last interviews. I did not know they were going to be so tough and rewarding. When I interviewed my mom and dad to find out more of my childhood stories that shaped who I am and what my brand is today, I unexpectedly discovered healing for myself and my family. Coming out as gay to my parents was a tough chapter in my life. These interviews were the first time I asked my parents how they felt about my gay identity and career choices. I did not expect them to cry or apologize for making bad decisions. Having these hard heart-to-heart conversations lifted a weight for my parents, because it gave them a chance to say things they had been holding back for over 15 years. It was a healing that made us feel closer and lighter.

Looking back, I realize they did the hardest thing a parent can do, but they still loved me even as they were struggling to accept my true identity. And yet it was the best thing that could have happened to me. I was forced to become independent, grow up, and become a man I could be proud of. I was so close to my family that this chapter of separation was key to accelerating my growth, stoking my hunger for entrepreneurship, and teaching me life skills they could not have taught me.

This book has been part of the best year of my life, in spite of the world struggling through a pandemic. I completed a full year of sobriety, and when I celebrated my first anniversary with my support group, a friend said she remembered that in my first meeting I was shaking in my seat, and she expressed pride in my transformation. Even my parents say they almost don't recognize me after this year of transformation. I am proud to say how much gratitude I have in my life and how much I have accomplished since getting this clarity. I am a different person now that I am not pushing through a fog.

My old self could get clouded by my ego and the pressure to fit in. Now, I truly appreciate the small things and see the bigger picture. I am so grateful that my loved ones are healthy. The old version of Ivan used to complain about working hard or just complained whenever someone asked me, "How are you?" Now, I respond with how well I'm doing. I keep a positive attitude and spread the good mood. People enjoy talking to me more, and they remark that I am helping them remember what is good in their own lives. This is how I want to be remembered, in a positive way, and that is part of my Brand with Purpose.

Breaking the chain

This book became a 360-degree mirror, reflecting myself from every angle. In order to ask you, my readers, to thoroughly examine yourselves, I needed to do the exercises I suggest in this book and learn to love and accept everything, especially what I thought was negative about myself and my journey. I was able to get rid of all the filters that were put in my life by bad experiences and finally shatter them once and for all. For example, I had to face the echoes of self-doubt and decide that the greater good of this project was more important than standing in anxiety, anticipating negative feedback or that people would not agree to an interview. I gained confidence by taking the risk of asking for interviews and being okay with the process. Sometimes people took longer to schedule an interview, and I was pleasantly surprised by the amount of positive feedback and support. With practice and by repeatedly taking risks, I broke through a false concept that I shouldn't ask for help. I dreamed big and got what I wanted to fill this book with great leaders to share with you.

I already know what other resources to develop to support you in your success. You are invited to dive deeper by joining me in my podcast series and to receive coaching through my video production course Brand with Video. The beginning of my next book, *Breaking the Chain*, will focus on helping you heal the cracks in your self-confidence and build your personal power. I know that my Swiss Army knife of personal growth tools, a synthesis of the self-help courses and professional conferences I have invested in, has more to offer than we could fit in this book.

By reading this book, you have begun to "brand with purpose." I often reread books or go back to review a favorite podcast. Sometimes I find a new insight just because I'm a different person than I was in the first pass. I hope you will not passively consume the ideas in this book, but rather actively engage with the stories, the case studies, the insights, the exercises. I want you to be the creator and driver of your journey, for your own fulfillment and for community impact. I don't want you to feel adrift or lost. There are so many ways to join my community and reach out for further support. This book is meant to challenge you, and I know you can forge your own routines to be more present and mindful. I want you to find your fire, your purpose, and to broadcast that brand effectively to the world.

You can "brand with purpose" no matter what your career path is. Journal, meditate, reflect. Every day. And you will find your footsteps, one by one, that will lead you to your success.

EXERCISES

- Are there certain exercises in this book that you would like to go back and review and highlight? Some exercises might be worth repeating to see if you have different answers now that you have worked through more exercises and more of a personal journey.

- What important lessons have you learned that will impact your brand or clarify your purpose?

- Did you get stuck or have difficulty with certain questions? How do you want to support yourself to get through those challenges? A coach, supportive peer, or weekly mastermind group?

- Are there people you want to interview that you haven't thought about interviewing before? Consider what questions you want to ask your parents, community leaders, former schoolteachers, or former bosses.

- Dream big. Who would you like to meet to grow your network that you didn't think you could reach? Who do you want to help you become your best self or build your brand? Look in your social network (or review some of the exercises in chapter 12 to grow your network) and ask them if they can help you make that dream connection!

- As I asked my interviewees at the end of each interview: What does "brand with purpose" mean to you?

ACKNOWLEDGMENTS

WRITING THIS book has been a journey in digging through my memories. My early years were so influenced by the love and support of my family. So I want to acknowledge first my mother and father, Maria and Luis, who were teachers by example, living the values of hard work, persistence, education, and always doing the right thing. They both made choices and sacrifices to give my sister and me the best possible life opportunities.

My biggest cheerleader and partner in crime, Vianett, has been more than a sister to me. We have shared so much laughter and love in the good times, and she stood by me as my rock during the tough times. Vianett has also brought Cassie and Luca as the new members of our family, who bring us so much joy. Luca, my sweet nephew, has given me the inspiration to write this book and dream of a world where he and a new generation can remember "you are never alone."

The passionate support from my extended family of over 50 cousins and almost 30 aunts and uncles helped me with research and ideas. They gave me confidence by saying they will be the first in line at the book launch party, including some flying in from Mexico.

My angels in the sky, my beautiful grandparents Max and Maria, Consuelo and Ricardo—I hear them whispering wisdom in my ear. Although our time together was short, I want my grandparents to be proud of me and know I remember them always. My grandfather Max, our family's leading businessman and mentor, shared his early vision of me as a future success by the gift of his Rolex designated in his will, and this gave me self-confidence when I was truly challenged in my early career.

My team of coaches and mentors have been invaluable to my personal growth and the design of a new life. My editor and creative consultant, Jen Cheng, helped bring out my ideas and stories to shape this book. She not only helped me realize a dream, but she also helped me discover gifts and strengths that I didn't know were possible. Some of my mentors have generously given their support for over a decade, and their advice has been invaluable to me: Aaron Keith, Robert Furse, Tony Svoboda, Jason Pantana, Rick Dergan, and Fran Hughes. Their leadership and belief in my abilities has reminded me of all that I am capable of and all that is possible.

My friends are my honest mirrors, and this inner circle has supported me through the roller coaster of life. These ride or die friends believed in the concept of this book and offered their help from the start: Candice Griego, Dean McCarthy, Imene Meziane, and Alek Duboff. Some of the interviewees and ideas in this book came from my conversations and informal brainstorming sessions with them. This book would not be possible without all the interviewees who generously shared their wisdom. These leaders are incredible people who inspire courage and persistence to live boldly.

My day-to-day work would not be possible without my hardworking teams supporting this book. It has been so reassuring to have the professional experience of the publishing team at Page Two to pull all the pieces together and boost this book's success. My team at "Brand With" is working tirelessly to create an ecosystem that supports creatives and entrepreneurs. Every member of Ivan Estrada Properties reminds me of the importance of teamwork, individual strength, and leadership growth.

My spiritual development has benefited from the quiet support of a companion who has been through all the twists and turns with me, my dog Noah, my favorite furry friend who has listened to my inner thoughts. My belief in my higher power has been a guiding light that has brought me to the development of this book and a vision to reach more entrepreneurs. For many years my faith was shaken and I thought I was forgotten. I now know that everything that I experienced was part of the process and I appreciate all those life lessons and all of those that are yet to come.

My readers are so important to the vision of this book. Thank you for taking the time to invest in yourself and engage with the wisdom I have gathered. I hope that your journey with this book empowers you to make your impact, efforts small or big, with more possibilities and color.

RESOURCES

1. What's Your Story?

Stanford University's Latino
Business Action Network
lban.us

Brand With
BrandWith.com

Chelsea Phaire
Alaa Elassar, "10-Year-Old Girl Has
Sent More Than 1,500 Art Kits to Kids
in Foster Care and Homeless Shelters
during the Coronavirus Pandemic,"
CNN.com, May 20, 2020, cnn.com/
2020/05/20/us/10-year-old-girl-art
-kits-foster-care-homeless-shelter
-trnd/index.html.

GT Dave
gtslivingfoods.com

Tom Foster, "Meet the King of
Kombucha," *Inc.*, March 2015, inc.com/
magazine/201503/tom-foster/the-king-
of-kombucha.html.

Jonathan Leary
remedyplace.com

"L.A. Parking Garage Gets New Life
as Wellness Oasis," *LoopNet*, January
9, 2020, loopnet.com/learn/la-parking
-garage-gets-new-life-as-wellness-oasis
-/1383313537/.

Jay Shetty
jayshetty.me

La Michoacana
la-michoacana.com/aboutus.html

Hussein Kalaoui, Stacey-Ann Johnson,
Nicole Karlisch, and Leeatt Rothschild,
"La Michoacana: The Story of an
Orphaned Brand," University of
Pennsylvania, *Knowledge@Wharton*,
April 20, 2009, knowledge.wharton.
upenn.edu/article/la-michoacana-the-
story-of-an-orphaned-brand.

Serena Maria Daniels, "The Paleta War," *Eater*, October 22, 2019, eater.com/2019/10/22/20908347/la-michoacana-paleta-legal-battle.

Sarah Culberson
sarahculberson.com

Melissa & Doug, toy company
melissaanddoug.com

2. Be Bold and Different

Wilson Cruz
instagram.com/wcruz73

Rick Bentley, "Wilson Cruz Key Part of LGBTQ History on TV," KGET. com, February 14, 2020, kget.com/community/ricks-reviews/wilson-cruz-key-part-of-lgbtq-history-on-tv.

GLAAD, "Wilson Cruz Joins GLAAD Staff," press release, September 4, 2012, glaad.org/releases/wilson-cruz-joins-glaad-staff.

Mark Batson
therealmarkbatson.com

Megan Rapinoe
Alison Beard, "Life's Work: An Interview with Megan Rapinoe," *Harvard Business Review*, July–August 2020, hbr.org/2020/07/lifes-work-an-interview-with-megan-rapinoe.

Trevor Moawad
Quotes from Optimize.me (website), optimize.me/quotes/trevor-moawad/1538963-a-few-years-into-our-time-working-together-i-showed.

Lizzo
Calin Van Paris, "Lizzo Wants to Redefine the Body-Positivity Movement," Vogue.com, September 24, 2020, vogue.com/article/lizzo-october-cover-story-body-positivity-inclusivity.

Humble Lukanga
Ashley Cullins, "How This Hollywood Business Manager Went from Escaping Genocide to Overseeing Opulence," *Hollywood Reporter*, October 16, 2018, hollywoodreporter.com/news/general-news/issa-raes-business-manager-survived-genocide-uganda-1150559.

Liz Marie
lizmariestrategy.com

3. Authenticity

Sobriety and mental health resources
soberish.co/the-17-best-online-sobriety-support-spaces-for-2021/
samhsa.gov/find-help/recovery
psychologytoday.com

SWOT analysis
businessnewsdaily.com/4245-swot-analysis.html

Cisco Home
ciscohome.net

Madam C.J. Walker
Self Made: Inspired by the Life of Madam C.J. Walker (TV series), netflix.com/title/80202462.

Tyrone McKinley Freeman, interviewed by Amanda B. Moniz, "Madam C.J. Walker's Philanthropy," *O Say Can You See?* (blog), National Museum of American History, Smithsonian Institution, March 27, 2018, americanhistory.si.edu/blog/walker.

Lizzie Velásquez
Lizzie Velásquez, "How Do You Define Yourself?" TEDxAustinWomen, December 2013, ted.com/talks/lizzie_velasquez_how_do_you_define_yourself.

Darryll Stinson
Darryll Stinson, "Overcoming Rejection: When People Hurt You and Life Isn't Fair," TEDxWileyCollege, October 2019, ted.com/talks/darryll_stinson_overcoming_rejection_when_people_hurt_you_life_isn_t_fair.

Robert Frost
Robert Frost, "The Road Not Taken," robertfrost.org/the-road-not-taken.jsp.

4. Invest in Yourself

Amy Cuddy
Amy Cuddy, "Your Body Language May Shape Who You Are," TEDGlobal 2012, June 2012, ted.com/talks/amy_cuddy_your_body_language_may_shape_who_you_are.

Meditation
awaken.com/2018/11/10-athletes-who-meditate

themindfulsteward.com/celebrities-and-athletes-who-meditate-everyday

learnrelaxationtechniques.com/free-guided-meditation-resources

uclahealth.org/marc

Aaron Keith
buildifysystems.com

Four Tendencies, Gretchen Rubin
quiz.gretchenrubin.com

Toastmasters
toastmasters.org

Mark Batson
therealmarkbatson.com

Vincent Jones
citizenjonestravel.com

5. Personalizing Video

Brand with Video course
BrandWith.com

María Elena Salinas
María Elena Salinas, "Raising My Hand in Spanish-Language Media," TEDxFoggyBottom, April 2018, ted.com/talks/maria_salinas_raising_my_hand_in_spanish_language_media.

cbsnews.com/team/maria-elena-salinas

hispanicmarketingcouncil.org/Events/Annual-Summit/Speakers-2018/Maria-Elena-Salinas

Janelle Monáe
Curt Nickisch, "Life's Work: An
Interview with Janelle Monáe,"
Harvard Business Review, September–
October 2020, hbr.org/2020/09/
lifes-work-an-interview-with-janelle-
monae.

Jorge Rivas, "Janelle Monáe on Being a
Former Maid and Why She Still Wears
a Uniform," *Colorlines*, November
5, 2012, colorlines.com/articles/
janelle-monae-being-former-maid-
and-why-she-still-wears-uniform.

David Beebe
davidbeebe.com

6. Social Media Influence

Wilson Cruz
instagram.com/wcruz73

Valentina Vee
valentinavee.com

Phil Lobel
lobeline.com/phil-lobel/

7. Building a Team, Expanding Your Brand

Jonathan Leary
remedyplace.com

DISC personality tests
truity.com/test/disc-personality-test
tonyrobbins.com/disc
discprofile.com/what-is-disc

HOTS personality
Mark Victor Hansen and Robert G.
Allen, *The One Minute Millionaire:
The Enlightened Way to Wealth* (New
York: Crown Publishing Group, 2002).

Myers–Briggs personality test
myersbriggs.org

Enneagram
enneagraminstitute.com/
type-descriptions

Appreciative Inquiry
David L. Cooperrider and Diana
Whitney, *Appreciative Inquiry:
A Positive Revolution in Change*
(Oakland, CA: Berrett-Koehler
Publishers, 2005).

davidcooperrider.com/ai-process

Brett Steenbarger, "Appreciative
Inquiry: Leading by Asking the
Right Questions," Forbes.com,
June 21, 2015, forbes.com/sites/
brettsteenbarger/2015/06/21/
appreciative-inquiry-leading-by-
asking-the-right-questions.

8. Packaging Product

Sharpe Suiting
sharpesuiting.com

Janelle Monáe
Jorge Rivas, "Janelle Monáe on Being a
Former Maid and Why She Still Wears
a Uniform," *Colorlines*, November
5, 2012, colorlines.com/articles/
janelle-monae-being-former-maid-
and-why-she-still-wears-uniform.

Compartés Chocolatier
compartes.com

Doyle Rice
instagram.com/royledice

Nicolette Jackson-Pownall
njpphotography.com

Tan France
Dressing Funny with Tan France
(trailer), YouTube.com, June 21, 2019,
youtube.com/watch?v=ywgO-mrX7Jw.

9. Finding Your Creativity

Mark Batson
therealmarkbatson.com

Austin Kleon
austinkleon.com

Questlove
Questlove, *Creative Quest* (New York:
Ecco Press, 2018).

questlove.com

Paul Mendoza
imdb.com/name/nm0579343

David Bamber
linkedin.com/in/
david-bamber-4854831a

Valentina Vee
valentinavee.com

10. Collaborations and Relationships

Phil Lobel
lobeline.com/phil-lobel/

Hoarders' Dorothy Breininger
aetv.com/shows/hoarders

Arturo Villarreal
virtusbuilding.com

Mark Batson
therealmarkbatson.com

Product placement
investopedia.com/terms/p/product-
placement.asp

Jon M. Chu
Michael Calore, "Jon M. Chu Shot This
Short Film Entirely on an iPhone XS
Max," Wired.com, September 19, 2018,
wired.com/story/jon-m-chu-short-
film-shot-on-iphone-xs-max.

Lulu Wang
Todd Spangler, "Apple Releases
Lulu Wang's Heartwarming Short
Film 'Nian' for Chinese New Year,
Shot Entirely on iPhone 12 Pro
Max," Variety.com, January 28, 2021,
variety.com/2021/digital/news/
apple-lulu-wang-nian-iphone-12-
chinese-new-year-1234895358.

Wang's film *Nian* can be seen here:
youtube.com/watch?v=t-9YuIg7R1I.

David Beebe
davidbeebe.com

11. Life's a Party

Phil Lobel
lobeline.com/phil-lobel/

Kyle Chan
kylechandesign.com

Nik Kacy
nikkacy.com

Equality Fashion Week
equalityfashionweek.com

Tom Ferry
tomferry.com

Evie Jeang
ideallegalgroup.com/evie-p-jeang

Electric Forest
electricforestfestival.com

Chad Hudson
chcre8tive.com

12. Networking and Philanthropy

Scott Turner
linkedin.com/in/scottthecareercoach

Malcolm Gladwell
Malcolm Gladwell, *The Tipping Point: How Little Things Can Make a Big Difference* (New York: Little, Brown, 2006).

Archetypes
Charlie Gilkey, "Maven, Connector, or Salesperson: What's Your Archetype?" *Productive Flourishing* (blog), April 4, 2012, productiveflourishing.com/maven-connector-or-salesperson-whats-your-archetype.

Imene Meziane
linkedin.com/in/
imene-meziane-3a583b77

Soho House
sohohouse.com

Mark Batson
therealmarkbatson.com

José Cabrera
josecabrera.com

thetherapystudio.org

Liz Marie Strategy
lizmariestrategy.com

Catherine An
houseofan.com

IKEA's Bully a Plant Project
Bradley Jolly, "Sense of Shelf: IKEA Asks Students to BULLY a Plant for 30 Days to See Whether It Withers... and the Results Were Incredible," *Sun* (UK), May 8, 2018, thesun.co.uk/news/6234065/IKEA-asks-students-bully-plant-negativity-stop-growth.

Random Acts of Kindness Foundation
randomactsofkindness.org

13. Create Content

Greg Berlanti
Sarah Rodman, "Hero's Journey: Greg Berlanti on His Two Decades of LGBTQ Inclusion," *Entertainment Weekly*, May 15, 2020, ew.com/tv/greg-berlanti-lgbtq-inclusion.

Chris Gardner, "Greg Berlanti Addresses Lesbian Batwoman Controversy: 'Ruby Is Terrific in the Role,'" *Hollywood Reporter*, October 8, 2018, hollywoodreporter.com/tv/tv-news/filmmaker-greg-berlanti-addresses-casting-ruby-rose-as-batwoman-1148612.

Anisha Manchanda
Nellie Andreeva, "Joel Stillerman's Content Superba Taps Anisha Manchanda as VP Development & Production," *Deadline*, July 27, 2020, deadline.com/2020/07/joel-stillerman-content-superba-taps-anisha-manchanda-vp-development-production-1202995835.

Padma Lakshmi
"*The New York Times*: Padma Lakshmi Finds a New Voice, Amplifying the Voices of Others," Padma (personal site), June 18, 2020, padmalakshmi.com/the-new-york-times-padma-lakshmi-finds-a-new-voice-amplifying-the-voices-of-others.

14. Pivoting
Kodak
Clare Duffy, "How Kodak Went from Photography Pioneer to Pharmaceutical Producer," CNN.com, August 4, 2020, cnn.com/2020/08/04/business/kodak-history-pharmaceutical-production/index.html.

Mark Batson
therealmarkbatson.com

David Beebe
davidbeebe.com

Belinda Carlisle
gogos.com/bio

Catherine An
houseofan.com

Vincent Jones
citizenjonestravel.com

Arturo Villarreal
virtusbuilding.com

Girlina/DJ Lina
Jasmin Hernandez, "Lina Bradford Impacts Audiences with Her Soulful DJ Sets and Her Selfless Activism," *Standard*, June 1, 2019, standardhotels.com/culture/lina_bradford_activism_pride.

Wayfair
Mark Wilson, "Wayfair's $112 Billion Plan to Take Over Your Entire Home," *Fast Company*, April 30, 2021, fastcompany.com/90626994/wayfairs-112-billion-plan-to-take-over-your-entire-home.

ABOUT THE AUTHOR

IVAN ESTRADA is an inspirational business leader and highly ranked real estate broker with extensive experience in the real estate and finance industries. He is a top producer in the Los Angeles metro area, with a thriving team in residential and commercial properties. Ivan is part of a selected cohort of leading entrepreneurs for the Stanford University Latino Entrepreneurship Initiative. He is a sought-after public speaker on the topics of branding and marketing, personal development, and real estate by organizations such as Inman, California Association of Realtors, and *The Real Deal*. He produces a large portfolio of video content, including the popular YouTube series *Real Estate Minute*. He has been featured on NBC's *Open House*, HGTV's *House Hunters*, and Bravo's *Million Dollar Listing*, as well as in *LA Times*, *Forbes*, *Hollywood Reporter*, and *Dwell*. He was named among the nation's top "30 Under 30" in real estate with the National Association of Realtors and is also regularly named in *Newsweek*'s America's Best Realtors list. He holds a bachelor's degree in finance and accounting from the University of Southern California and is a CPA. Ivan is currently a member of the Advisory Council at the Natural History Museum of Los Angeles County and was a former president of the Los Angeles LGBTQ Chamber of Commerce. Ivan is a tenor, known as a teen singer on variety shows for Univision and TV Azteca. He is a proud uncle and loves to take his cockapoo dog, Noah, running on the beach.

WANT TO KEEP BRANDING WITH ME?

Brand With ecosystem

If you enjoyed the lessons and stories in *Brand with Purpose*, I've got something to tell you! This book is only one part of the Brand With ecosystem. Brand with Video is an online, interactive personal development, business growth, and video marketing course that I have put together to teach people how to leverage themselves to increase their sales and brand awareness.

Brand With Podcast

Brand With Podcast is an aspirational and inspirational podcast where I host diverse, highly successful guests as we dissect their careers through a branding and marketing lens. I created this ecosystem to get you started on making the necessary lifestyle and business changes to become successful and to support you on the path to fulfilling your potential. If you want to learn more about the Brand With ecosystem, you can check out the links below.

BrandWith.com

instagram.com/therealbrandwith

facebook.com/therealbrandwith

youtube.com/c/brandwith

linkedin.com/company/brand-with

Listen to the *Brand With Podcast* by Ivan Estrada, available on all the major streaming platforms: ivanestrada.com/podcast.

Looking for a home?

I am a licensed CPA who is currently working as a top real estate broker in Los Angeles, California. I have found that part of my purpose is helping people find houses that they can call their homes. If you are interested in looking for a home in the Greater Los Angeles area, you can contact me using the links below.

ivanestradaproperties.com

ivanestrada.com

instagram.com/ivanestradaproperties

facebook.com/IvanEstradaRE

youtube.com/ivanestradaproperties

linkedin.com/in/ivanestradaproperties

twitter.com/ivanestradahome